# Mastering Webcam and Smartphone Video:

# How to Look and Sound Great in Webinars and Videoconferences

**By Jan Ozer**

**Doceo**
Publishing, Inc.

# Mastering Webcam and Smartphone Video:
# How to Look and Sound Great in Webinars and Videoconferences

Jan Ozer

Doceo Publishing
412 West Stuart Drive
Galax, VA 24333

www.doceo.com
www.thewebcambook.com

**ISBN: 978-0-9762595-6-5**

Printed in the United States of America

To Barbara, Whatley and Eleanor

For loaning me your stuff

and

To Anthony Q. Artis

For the inspiration (to shut up and write)

# Acknowledgments

I couldn't have written this book without the backing of the Streaming Media team, for the seminars and webinars that they've sponsored, the contacts that they've fostered, and the various writing assignments that helped me become familiar with the products and technologies discussed herein. So to Eric Schumacher-Rasmussen, Stephen Nathans-Kelly, Troy Dreier, Dan Rayburn, Joel Unickow, Dick Kaser, and Tom Hogan Jr. and Sr., thank you, thank you, thank you.

I also want to express my appreciation to the vendors who have provided hardware, software, access to their platforms, and bountiful assistance, including Adobe, Apple, Azden, HP, IK Multimedia, Livestream, Logitech, Matrox, MediaPlatform, NewTek, Onstream, Panasonic, Panopto, PreSonus, Sonic Foundry, TalkPoint, Telestream, Teradek, Total Webcasting, Ustream, and VideoGuys, and I'm sure some that I've forgotten.

This book is the fifth published by my company, Doceo Publishing. As always, budgets are tight, time is short, and the topics are fast moving, so I apologize in advance for any rough edges. Any polish that you see is wholly attributable to my copy editor/proofreader Lucy Sutton, and cover designer extraordinaire, Becky White.

As always, thanks to Pat Tracy for technical and marketing assistance.

# Contents

# Contents

# Introduction: We Were All Media Novices Once

I remember the first time I was on national TV with agonizing clarity. It was early fall, and Microsoft had just launched a new version of Windows. I was a contributing editor for *PC Magazine*, and one of the networks called for an interview. I agreed.

The weekend before the call, I had spent a sweaty couple of days working in the yard in the steamy Atlanta sun. For relief that Monday, I had gone to the barber and had my head shaved. Bad move—the next day, the network called.

The appearance was for the national evening news, and I drove to the local affiliate in Atlanta. The studio was totally dark in the break between the 5 PM and 11 PM news, and it was just me, the lights, and a camera person, with an earpiece though which I heard the director in New York City.

I looked like a cross between a white supremacist and a deer caught in the headlights of an oncoming tractor trailer. My performance was predictably dismal. The only positive note was that this was pre-Internet, so my 15 minutes of fame were just that, 15 minutes. The only people who saw me were those unfortunate enough to be watching the news that night. But I vowed, never again.

I produced my first video training series soon thereafter, but only after weeks of media training. Then I bought the first of many video cameras and started producing videos. First, it was the typical family stuff, but this transitioned to concerts and conventions, marketing videos, advertorials and advertisements, and more training videos.

During this period, the Internet happened. My primary technical focus has always been video compression, the enabling technology for all video on the Internet. Webinars, essentially the intersection of live video and the Internet, became a natural extension. Over the last five or six years, I've produced dozens of webinars on both sides of the camera, and have reviewed most of the major conferencing and webinar production systems. Along the way, I've written 20 or so books on some aspect of video production or compression.

Nice history, but why should you care? Because let's face it: although webcams and smartphones make video more accessible for business and pleasure, simply owning one doesn't make you a video expert. While webinars and videoconferencing can be fabulous business tools, you have to look and sound professional to achieve a positive result. Trust me: if you look and perform like I did back in that dark studio, your result will be anything but positive.

Overall, to produce high-quality video with a webcam or smartphone, you need to understand audio and video production from both sides of the camera, you have to know a bit about video compression, and you must be familiar with the operation of conferencing and webinar software. All this is what you will learn from this book, which is divided into five major parts.

## Section I: Quick Start

The Quick Start contains visual lessons primarily from Section II: Looking Great. They're a lead-in to the content covered in Section II and a quick reminder you can use before any webinars or conferences that you produce.

## Section II: Looking Great

The first chapter is on bandwidth, or your connection speed to the Internet. You'll learn how much you need, how to measure how much you have, and what happens if you don't have enough.

Subsequent chapters focus on producing the highest possible video quality. Chapter 2 discusses positioning your webcam, which is where you'll learn classic production techniques like the rule of thirds and proper framing.

Chapter 3 is about choosing your background, and Chapter 4 choosing your clothing, both of which can have a dramatic affect on video quality. You'll learn about lighting in Chapter 5, and see how investing $30 in a clamp light can have a positive impact on your presentation. In Chapter 6, you'll learn how to optimize video quality when your webcam's auto settings just won't do. After finishing this section, your video will look great, and it'll be time to think about audio.

## Section III: Sounding Great

While we spend most of our time focusing on how we look on camera, the most important information is passed via audio. Although most web viewers will excuse blocky or grainy video, their expectations are higher for audio. So it's critical to get this right.

Using the integrated microphone on your computer, webcam, or smartphone, is seldom, if ever, the best option. In Chapter 7, you'll learn how to choose an external microphone (mic), and in Chapter 8, you'll learn how to use it.

In Chapter 9, you'll learn some critical audio fundamentals that will allow you to connect and set microphone volume. This chapter is essential to the four that follow, which detail how to connect and set up a mic in Windows (Chapter 10), on the Mac (Chapter 11), on iOS devices (Chapter 12), and Android devices (Chapter 13). I know you're going to want to jump right to your platform of choice, but you should read Chapters 7 to 9 first to learn the basics.

## Section IV: How it Works in the Programs You Use

To keep the chapters in Section II and III as focused as possible, I include minimal application-specific information. In Chapter 14, you'll learn how to optimize audio and video quality on the Mac and iOS devices when conferencing with FaceTime. Chapter 15 details Google Hangouts operation on four platforms (Windows/Mac/iOS/Android), while Chapter 16 does the same for GoToWebinar, Chapter 17 tackles On24 Webcast Elite, Chapter 18 addresses Onstream Webinars, Chapter 19 discusses Skype, Chapter 20 covers TalkPoint Convey, while Chapter 21 details audio and video operations in WebEx.

## Section V: Getting it Right on Game Day

This section contains one eponymous chapter, which includes a number of production-related checklists to ensure the best possible event.

If you invest the time to read these chapters and then apply your new knowledge, you will look and sound great during webinars and videoconferences. As a result, you'll present with more confidence and achieve better results.

While novice users will gain the most benefit from this book, even experienced webcam pros will find multiple nuggets of value.

# What's on the Website?

The website www.thewebcambook.com accompanies this book. Note the "the" in the URL, as plain www.webcambook.com is a free sex chat site. While I'm sure it has its charms, I want to make sure you find the right site.

At this point, to be honest, the website is a work in progress. It will contain a few items referenced within these pages from the start, with additional materials added over time. So check it out and let me know what you think at jan@thewebcambook.com.

# Quick Start: Do This, Don't Do That

**Do this**          **Don't do that**

*Figure a. Check your upload speed well in advance; don't just pray for the best.*

This chapter contains highlights from various chapters in the book, both as a quick-start reference and as an introduction to the materials covered in the book.

As you can see in Figure a, it's better to check your outbound bandwidth with a tool called Speedtest than to simply pray that your bandwidth is sufficient. Chapter 1 has tables detailing the recommended bitrate for various conferencing and webinar applications, and other, related tips. Note that Speedtest is available as an app for both iOS and Android platforms, so you can check there as well.

# Camera Positioning and Lighting

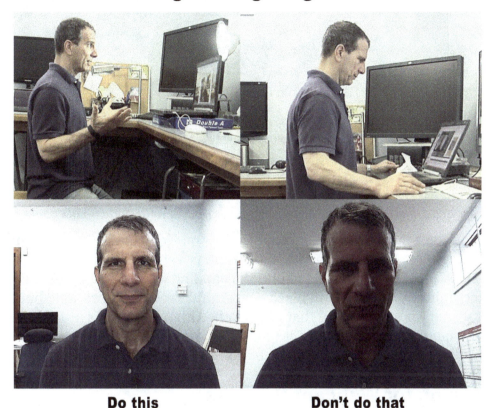

**Do this**          **Don't do that**

*Figure b. Position the webcam at eye level.*

If you're conferencing from the webcam on your computer, chances are the lens is much lower than eye level. This looks bad (nose hairs are a definite turn-off) and causes a range of problems—including the backlighting and resulting dark video shown on the lower right of Figure b. While you can fix backlighting with your webcam software, the best option is to avoid the problem altogether and position the camera at eye level.

Throw in the clamp light used on the upper left, and you get excellent exposure and quality, all for about $30. Chapter 2 discusses camera positioning and framing, while Chapter 5 details lighting options. You'll learn how to fix backlighting (when you can't avoid it) in Chapter 6.

## Choosing a Background

**Do this**                    **Don't do that**

*Figure c. Don't use a reflective gray background with wide open spaces.*

Your background can have a profound affect on video quality, as you can see in Figure c. The background on the right is a slightly reflective gray with too much open space, which enables the banding you can see in the image on the right. White, blue and black backgrounds seem to work well, but the best strategy is a studio like that on the left. Although there is little sharp detail, there's also no open spaces for video artifacts to run wild. You'll learn all the rules about choosing a background in Chapter 3.

## Dressing for Webcam Success

**Do this**                    **Don't do that (please)**

*Figure d. Excessive tiny detail in clothing or background
can produce awful results. Solid is always safest.*

On the left in Figure d, the subject wore a solid-colored shirt and a solid-colored sweater. If the background was reddish, he could have removed the sweater and the shirt would have worked just fine.

The gentleman on the right wore a blue pinstriped shirt that reacted very poorly with the compression used in all Internet video. The result was mushy detail and obvious moiré patterns. You can get away with thick patterns, but solids are always best. You can read up on more rules of dressing for webcam success in Chapter 4.

## Lighting for the Webcam

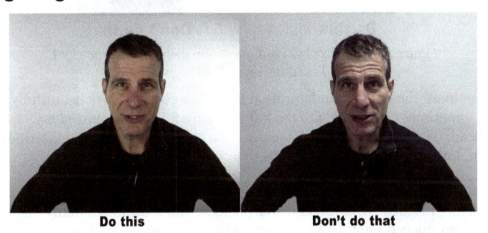

**Do this**          **Don't do that**

*Figure e. Ceiling lights only on the right, ceiling plus supplemental lighting on the left.*

The video on the right in Figure e was shot solely using overhead fluorescent lights. As a result, the forehead (and wrinkles thereupon) are well lit, but the bottom of the face is too dark. On the left, I added lights in front and in back, producing better skin tones and more even lighting across the face.

Adding even a couple of clamp lights to the mix can really improve webcam quality—for under $60. You'll learn all about lighting in Chapter 5.

## Fine-tuning Your Webcam Settings

**Do this**                    **Don't do that**

*Figure f. On the left I've configured my webcam; on the right,*
*I used the default settings.*

Sometimes, the default configuration used by webcams work beautifully, but sometimes they don't. On the left in Figure f, I've customized my webcam configuration with a Mac program called Webcam Settings; on the right, I'm using the default settings.

Most Windows-based webcams come with applications that let you configure brightness, color, and sharpness settings, although many Mac-based products do not. However, with Macs, you can use a third-party program like Webcam Settings to adjust your settings. In Chapter 6, you learn how to acquire Webcam Settings (or other programs), and more importantly, how to optimize your settings with a variety of programs.

## Producing High-quality Audio

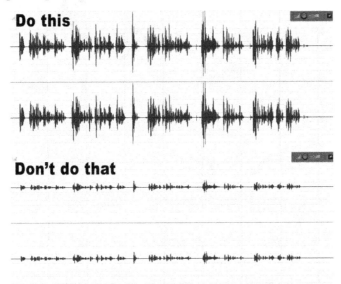

*Figure g. The audio represented by the waveform on the bottom would be pretty much inaudible.*

The most important information in virtually all videoconferences and webinars is carried by the audio, not the video. And the microphones on computers and webcams, in particular, are substandard. So you have to take great care to make sure your audio sounds like the waveform on top in Figure g, rather than on the bottom.

In Chapter 7, you'll learn which microphone to buy, and in Chapter 8, you'll learn how to use it. Chapter 9 includes fundamentals that help you understand what your target volume should be (think top of Figure g), while Chapters 10 through 13 detail how to connect your mic and adjust volume in Windows and on the Mac, and on iOS and Android mobile devices.

OK, that's the Quick Start. I hope it whets your appetite for what awaits you inside.

# Chapter 1: It's All About the Bandwidth

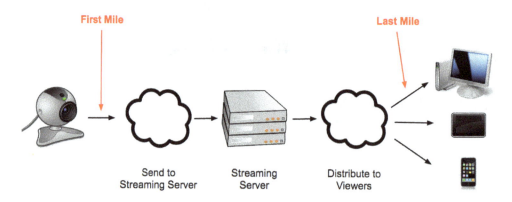

*Figure 1-1. All live events involve two critical bandwidths called the first and the last mile.*

Understanding and managing the bandwidths that control your conference or webinar are critical to audio and video quality and can make the difference between a successful event and an abject (and embarrassing) failure.

In this chapter, you'll learn what bandwidth is and how it affects your event. You'll also learn how to measure your bandwidth, and how much bandwidth you need to successfully produce your event.

# Overview

Did you ever produce (or watch) a video call or webinar that went horribly wrong, with frequent interruptions or perhaps a full stop or two? Yeah, me neither (wink, wink). In this chapter, you'll learn why these problems occur and, more importantly, how to avoid them. Specifically, you'll learn:

- What bandwidth is and why it's important

- What video compression is and why it's important

- How to measure your bandwidth

- How much bandwidth you need for conferencing, live streaming, and webinar events

- How to make sure you have enough working bandwidth for your conferencing event.

Let's get started.

# Defining Bandwidth

When I say bandwidth, I mean your connection speed to the Internet, which is often referred to as the cloud. As shown in Figure 1-1, there are two bandwidths that affect videoconferencing or webinar quality. The first mile, which you control, is where the video is transmitted from your computer or smartphone to the Internet. The last mile, which your viewer controls, is where your remote viewer retrieves the video. In between is the streaming server supplied by your service provider, working behind the scenes to manage the flow of video from sender to receiver.

First-mile bandwidth depends upon multiple factors. Some common scenarios would be:

• If you're FaceTime-ing from your iPhone without a Wi-Fi connection, your bandwidth is dictated by your cellular connection. 3G is sketchy; 4G is better but still not perfect.

•  If Skype-ing from a computer or notebook at work, your bandwidth is the connection speed of your office's local area network (LAN) to the Internet—or more importantly, your share of that connection.

• If videoconferencing from home, it's the speed of your home Internet connection—or again, your share of that connection. If Junior is uploading video to YouTube during your event, the result might not be pretty.

First-mile bandwidth is critical because it's how your video gets to the cloud. Conferences are real-time events, and if the video doesn't get uploaded in real time, it may simply stop. Or, because excess compression (explained next page) may be applied to facilitate the upload, your video may start looking blocky and ugly.

Simply stated, if your bandwidth is plentiful, you can produce very high-quality audio and video, even with a $30 webcam or inexpensive mobile phone. If your bandwidth is inadequate, the best A/V gear in the world won't help. So the first thing you should think about when producing any event, whether a simple Skype call or an expensive webinar, is to check your bandwidth. I'll show you how in a moment, but let's first take a quick look at compression.

## About Video Compression

Speaking of YouTube, if you've ever uploaded video to the site, you know that it can seemingly take forever. That's because video files are inherently very large. For this reason, any time you see video playing anywhere—whether it's a smartphone or computer, or even on a TV via cable or satellite—it's been compressed to simplify transport and storage.

More to the point, when you transmit video via a webcam, under the hood, the conferencing or other software is compressing the video. It's compressing the audio too, of course, but audio files are much smaller than video, and much easier to handle.

*Figure 1-2. This video is ugly because it's been overly compressed.*

The compression technologies applied to video are "lossy," which means the more you compress, the more quality you lose. Because satellite and cable channels have so much bandwidth, you seldom see blocky artifacts in the video, but you've probably noticed them in the past. When streaming over the Internet, however, bandwidths are much lower than cable or satellite, particularly via 3G or 4G wireless connections, or even Wi-Fi.

If you see blocky video like that in Figure 1-2 during your conferences, or if the video stops and starts, it's almost certainly because your connection speed to the Internet is too slow. You'll learn the bandwidth requirements of various programs below; but first, let's learn how to measure your bandwidth.

## What's a Codec?

If you've worked in and around compression-related technologies, you've probably heard the word codec. Codec is the contraction of COmpression/DECompression (or enCOde/DECode, depending on who you ask) and a codec is simply an audio or video compression technology. Most webcams use the H.264 video codec, and AAC audio codecs, which are international standards.

# Measuring Your Bandwidth

OK, bandwidth is important—you get it. How do you know how much bandwidth you have?

From your browser, navigate to www.speedtest.net and run the test. Or search in the iOS or Android App stores for Speedtest and install that. In Figure 1-3, you see the results achieved via my Comcast cable modem connection, which is actually pretty impressive for a small town in southwest Virginia.

*Figure 1-3. Speedtest is a critical tool for all live event producers.*

What do the numbers mean? Here's an explanation from the Speedtest site.

• The ping is the reaction time of your connection—how fast you get a response after you've sent out a request. A fast ping means a more responsive connection, especially in applications where timing is everything (like video games). Ping is measured in milliseconds (ms).

• The download speed is how fast you can pull data from the server to you. Most connections are designed to download much faster than they upload, since the majority of online activity, like loading web pages or streaming videos, consists of downloads. Download speed is measured in megabits per second (Mbps).

• The upload speed is how fast you send data from you to others. Uploading is necessary for sending big files via email, or for using video chat to talk to someone else online (since you have to send your video feed to them). Upload speed is measured in megabits per second (Mbps).

In short, if you're gaming, you care about ping. If you're watching video, you care about download speed. If you're broadcasting video, you care about upload speed.

### Download is Usually Faster than Upload

In most home Internet connections, download speed is much faster than upload speed. As an example, prior to the Comcast connection shown in Figure 1-3, my previous connection was only 800 kbps upload, 10 Mbps download. The download speed was fine for everyone except my gamer daughter, but the upload speed with inadequate for most conferencing and webinar productions. As you'll see in Table 1-1, the upload requirements for most conferencing apps are modest. Still, if you plan on producing lots of conferences, faster is definitely better.

## How Much Bandwidth Do You Need?

Now that you know the concept, let's see how much bandwidth you'll actually need. As you would expect, this depends upon the program that you're using as well as your configuration, with different requirements for the resolution and the number of participants. Table 1-1 contains the specs for several popular personal conferencing products including Skype, FaceTime and Oovoo, as provided by the developers on their website.

| Personal conferencing | Minimum Bandwidth | | Recommended Bandwidth | | Source |
|---|---|---|---|---|---|
| | Upload - Calling | Download - Watching | Upload - Calling | Download - Watching | |
| **Skype** | | | | | bit.ly/skype_bw |
| Calling | 30 kbps | 30 kbps | 100 kbps | 100 kbps | |
| Video Calling/Screen Sharing | 128 kbps | 128 kbps | 300 kbps | 300 kbps | |
| Video Calling (HQ) | 400 kbps | 400kbps | 500 kbps | 500 kbps | |
| Video Calling (HD) | 1.2 Mbps | 1.2 Mbps | 1.5 Mbps | 1.5 Mbps | |
| **FaceTime for Mac** | 1 Mbps | 1 Mbps | Not Specified | Not Specified | bit.ly/FTMac_BW |
| **FaceTime for iOS** | Not Specified | Not Specified | Not Specified | Not Specified | |
| **Oovoo** | | | | | bit.ly/Ooovo_BW |
| Single Caller | 230 kbps | 178 kbps | Not Specified | Not Specified | |
| Additional Callers | | 128 kbps/per person | Not Specified | Not Specified | |

*Table 1-1. Here are the bandwidth requirements
for several popular personal conferencing programs.*

With FaceTime, Apple tells you what's needed for video calling on a Mac (1 Mbps up and down), but doesn't provide similar guidance for iOS devices like iPhones, iPads and iPod touches. Oovoo's website reveals that the program will use more bandwidth when available to improve video quality; whether the other two programs do the same is unclear. Basically, if you're using any of these tools for business, you should visit the URLs listed in the table and read up on how much bandwidth you need for optimum quality.

## Kilobits, Megabits, and Gigabits

You probably know this, but let's be clear.
• kbps is kilobits per second, which is 1,000 bits.
• Mbps is megabits per second, or 1000 times faster than kbps.
• Gbps is gigabits per second, or 1000 times faster than Mbps.

This can get confusing, because 1.2 Mbps is the same speed as 1200 kbps. Just pay attention to the k or M or G and you should be OK.

Note that it takes 8 bits to make on byte. Telecommunications speeds are always in kilo, mega or giga**bits** per second, while storage mediums like hard drives and SD cards are in mega or giga**bytes**. Bytes are abbreviated in caps, like MB, which can be confusing. Just remember; if the number relates to transmission speed, it's almost always bits.

## Conferencing Products

Group conferencing products work similarly to the personal conferencing, with requirements depending upon video resolution and the number of participants. Table 1-2 shows the bandwidth requirements for several group conferencing products.

| Group Conferencing | Minimum Bandwidth | | Recommended Bandwidth | | Source |
|---|---|---|---|---|---|
| | Upload - Calling | Download - Watching | Upload - Calling | Download - Watching | |
| **Google Hangouts** | | | | | bit.ly/GHang_BW |
| 1:1 Connections | Not Specified | Not Specified | 1 Mbps | 1 Mbps | |
| Group Video Connectivity | Not Specified | Not Specified | 1 Mbps | 2 Mbps | |
| **Adobe Connect** | 512 kbps | 512 kbps | Not Specified | Not Specified | bit.ly/AConnect_BW |
| **GoToMeeting** | Not Specified | Not Specified | 1 Mbps | 1 Mbps | bit.ly/GTM_bw |
| **Cisco WebEx** | | | | | bit.ly/WebX_BW |
| 90p (160x90) | 0 kbps | Not Specified | 120 kbps | Not Specified | |
| 180p (320x180) | 120 kbps | Not Specified | 360 kbps | Not Specified | |
| 360p (640x360) | 360 kbps | Not Specified | 1200 kbps | Not Specified | |
| 720p (1280x720) | 1200 kbps | Not Specified | 2000 kbps | Not Specified | |
| **Microsoft Lync** | Varied | | | | bit.ly/MSLync_BW |

*Table 1-2. Bandwidth requirements for personal conferencing programs.*

For the most part, the requirements are straightforward, although those for Microsoft Lync were too complex to easily summarize within a table. Check the URL shown for more information.

## Live Streaming Products

You'll use one of the conferencing systems discussed above for most webcam productions, but I've run several on live streaming services like Livestream and YouTube Live to good effect. These products operate differently from conferencing products. Specifically, rather than having a set bandwidth requirement for a specific window size, these tools let you send the highest possible signal your available bandwidth will support.

This is shown in Figure 1-4. As you can see, if you have between 3,000 and 6,000 kbps, YouTube Live will stream a 1080p video with a resolution of 1920 x 1080. If you have between 1500 and 4000 kbps, YouTube Live will stream at 720p, which is 1280 x 720. When using services like YouTube

Live, check your bandwidth with a tool like Speedtest and choose the appropriate bandwidth when you configure your project.

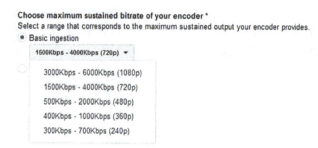

*Figure 1-4. Services like YouTube Live will take as much bandwidth as you can deliver.*

## Video Resolution and Bitrate

Most current webcams are high definition (HD). This means they capture an image that's at least 1280 x 720, which means 1280 pixels wide, and 720 pixels high. These width and height numbers are known as a video's resolution. A resolution of 1280 x 720 is called 720p, as you can see in Figure 1-4. Full HD is 1920 x 1080, or 1080p. In both, the p stands for progressive, rather than interlaced, which is way too complicated to get into here.

While bigger is always better, it also takes a higher data rate (defined below) to maintain the same quality. You can see the required bitrate drop with the resolutions shown in Figure 1-4, from 3000 to 6000 kbps (same as 3 to 6 Mbps) for 1080p video, down to 300 to 700 kbps for 240p video, which is 420 x 240 resolution.

Think of bandwidth as a small can of paint. If you try to paint a small area of the wall, things look great. If you try to paint the whole wall, coverage gets sketchy and the job looks awful. So if you only have 1 Mbps of upload bandwidth, it's better to use a smaller resolution like 360p (640 x 360) rather than 480p (854 x 480) or larger.

## Webinar Services

Webinar services operate in one of two ways. Most inexpensive services, like GoToWebinar and WebEx, operate like conferencing systems, requiring some minimal bandwidth but not upgrading quality when additional bandwidth is available. Some higher-end systems operate like live streaming service providers and accept the highest-quality signal you can send. So before producing a webinar, check with your service provider to understand how they work and how much bandwidth is required.

*When it comes to one-to-many conferencing, you have multiple options. That is, you can use a live streaming service provider like YouTube Live or Livestream, a webcasting service like Onstream or TalkPoint, or a conferencing service like GoToMeeting. Which is best? I explore this topic in an article you can find at bit.ly/wc_platform.*

## Bandwidths and Bitrates

As you've learned, bandwidth is the capacity of your Internet connection to deliver video to and from the Internet. Bitrate is a different, but related concept.

Specifically, whenever you videoconference, the conferencing software—whether Skype, FaceTime or other—compresses the live video stream behind the scenes. When this happens, the program has to compress that stream to a specific bitrate (or data rate). This is the amount of audio/video data in the file for any given second, whether 500 kbps or 2 Mbps.

When the bitrate of the video file is smaller than your upload bandwidth to the Internet (the first mile), video delivery to the Internet is smooth and uninterrupted. When the bitrate of your file exceeds your first mile bandwidth, bad things happen. Either the video stops completely, or the program applies more compression so the video fits, often causing the blockiness shown in Figure 1-2.

# Other Bandwidth Rules

Now that you know the basics, let's look at how to apply them.

## Budget Twice Your Actual Requirements

When you're booked on a flight leaving at 3 PM, you typically don't appear at the gate at 2:59—or at least I don't. Rather, you leave yourself some wiggle room to account for traffic jams and the inevitable long lines at security checkpoints. So it is with conferencing and bandwidth.

All connections to the Internet fluctuate in terms of capacity; in fact, the Internet itself is in a constant state of flux. For this reason, when conference, you should try to make sure that you have 2 times the bandwidth of your actual requirements.

That is, if you're video conferencing via Facetime, be sure you have 2 Mbps of outbound bandwidth, not the requested 1 Mbps. If you're working with YouTube Live, and Speedtest tells you that you have 6 Mbps of outbound bandwidth, choose the 1500 to 4000 kbps (720p) connection, not the 3000 to 6000 kbps (1080p) connection. That way, your high-quality signal will continue to go through even during the expected and unavoidable bandwidth fluctuations.

Any webcasting pro will tell you it's better to deliver a consistent lower-quality stream than a higher-quality stream with frequent interruptions. They'll also tell you that you can never have too much first mile bandwidth.

## If it's Shared, Be Scared

I know, corny, right? "If the glove doesn't fit, you must acquit" (do people even say corny anymore?). Don't let that detract from the message, however, which is never use shared bandwidth for mission-critical video conferencing calls or broadcasts.

Say you're at the airport and you run Speedtest in the US Air or Delta lounge. Bandwidth looks plentiful, so you start your video call. Then the flight from Dallas comes in and 20 additional video calls start up. Since your bandwidth is shared, you get increasingly smaller allocations until the call drops altogether. Not good.

I had a similar experience at a local concert that I streamed live. The phone company was a sponsor and guaranteed an upload speed of 25 to 30 Mbps, which I confirmed while testing a few days before the event. When I expressed concern about the bandwidth being accessible via Wi-Fi to attendees, they pooh-poohed my concerns and assured me that the outbound bandwidth would be sufficient.

I reran Speedtest about 30 minutes before show time, and the available bandwidth was below 1 Mbps and varying wildly. I convinced the phone company to disable Wi-Fi, and since I was connected via Ethernet, outbound bandwidth great. Had they not reversed course, my attempts at live streaming would have been a disaster. The obvious lesson is that even when bandwidth is plentiful, if it's shared, there's no guarantee that you'll get the bandwidth that you need. If you have a mission-critical video call or webinar coming up, here are some tips to consider:

- In a big office setting, ask your network administrators if they can reserve bandwidth for your event.

- If you're small business with just a few employees, make sure none start to upload videos to YouTube (or other bandwidth-hogging activities) during your call.

- If you're in a hotel or conference center and the call or event is truly mission-critical, provision your own dedicated bandwidth (check at the front desk or with the conference facilities). The costs are outrageous, but it's the best way to ensure that the call goes through.

## 3G? 4G?

3G and 4G are designations for generation of cellular equipment, with 3G third generation and 4G the fourth. Although you'll seldom achieve the theoretical maximums, 3G is designed to deliver 2 Mbps upload speed while moving and 28 Mbps while stationary, while 4G is designed to deliver 100 Mbps while moving and up to 1 Gbps while stationary.

OpenSignal (opensignal.com) tracks the real-world 2G, 3G, and 4G performance around the world and can even show where towers are located. Here's what the site told me about 4G bandwidth around the Big Apple in April 2015.

*Figure 1-5. OpenSignal ratings in New York City.*

## Be cautious about 4G

While 4G can be a great solution, at the end of the day, it's a shared resource as well. That is, the phone company has a fixed outbound capacity from the cell tower to the central office. If you're the only 4G connection hitting the tower, you should get more than the capacity you need. But if a bunch of other folks start broadcasting, they may overwhelm the bandwidth from the tower to the central office (see Figure 1-6).

In addition, as we all have experienced, 4G connection speed varies widely from location to location—or even at the same location at different times. This uncertainty is fine for casual FaceTime calls with a buddy, but not acceptable for important conferences or webinars. In most instances, for mission-critical conferences, try to find a high-quality Wi-Fi connection rather than using 4G.

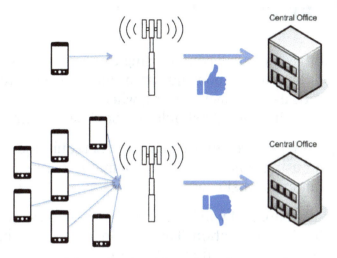

*Figure 1-6. 4G is great, but it's a shared connection as well.*

## Favor Ethernet Cable Over Wi-Fi

Many times, in an office or even conference setting, you'll have the option to use either Wi-Fi or a direct-wired connection. While Wi-Fi is generally easier, a cabled connection is generally more reliable.

The non-technical explanation is that interference can cause problems with Wi-Fi connections. If you need a more detailed explanation, check out an article entitled "Why Wi-Fi is Bad for Video" in *TV Technology* Magazine (bit.ly/cableoverwifi). You'll never use Wi-Fi for conferencing again.

> **tip** *If you do connect your computer to the Internet via a cable, remember to disconnect or shut off your Wi-Fi connection to make sure you're using the cabled connection.*

# Key Takeaways

• Bandwidth is life for all conferencing events; no bandwidth, no event. Poor bandwidth, poor-quality event. Whenever you plan a mission-critical conferencing event, whether a FaceTime call or webinar, your first thought should be about bandwidth.

• All applications have differing bandwidth requirements and schemes for using bandwidth. Before a mission-critical event, you should read up on what's required.

• Try to make sure that you have access to two times the bandwidth required by your application. That should allow you to handle any large drops in bandwidth during the call.

• Avoid shared bandwidth whenever possible. In an office setting, be sure to reserve bandwidth from your IT folks for mission-critical events.

• Be cautious about using single-mode 4G, as it can be unreliable.

• When both cabled connection and Wi-Fi are available, use the cable.

# Chapter 2: Positioning Your Webcam

*Figure 2-1. Eye to eye with my Logitech webcam (atop the Mac monitor).*

People watch professionally produced video on TV all day long. How the subject is positioned within the video frame is dictated by several key rules and principles.

Follow these, and your video looks professional too. Ignore them, and your video will look noticeably off to most viewers—even if they don't know why. Fortunately, these rules are pretty simple. In about 10 minutes, you'll be ready to go.

# Overview

As the snappy introduction suggested, this chapter will teach you where to place your webcam or smartphone/tablet and how to position yourself within the video frame. It's a short, fun chapter that will make you the director of your own webcam productions—and in the process change the way you look at your, and other people's, webcam videos. Specifically, in this chapter, you will learn:

- Why it's important to use a camera at eye level
- What the rule of thirds is and how to conform to it
- What framing is, and what the rules are.

At the end of the chapter, I discuss how you can use a traditional camcorder instead of a webcam. Let's get started.

# Getting Started

*Figure 2-2. President Kennedy in perfect rule-of-thirds positioning.*
*(Photo courtesy National Archives.)*

President Kennedy was the first media-savvy president, and the only president I could think of who wouldn't potentially polarize a significant group of readers. The video shown in Figure 2-2, shot back in 1963, shows that the cameraman (almost certainly a man back then) knew what he was doing.

## Use an Eye-level Camera Angle

What can we take from this frame grab? First, it's clear that the camera is at eye-level—it's not shooting down at the President from above, or up from below. Unfortunately, since most webcams on notebooks and mobile devices are well below eye level, you have to work hard to achieve the same camera angle when conferencing with these devices. For many reasons, this hard work is worth it.

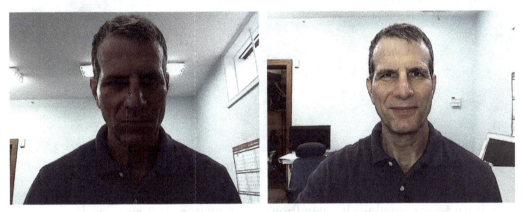

*Figure 2-3. Low-angle versus eye level shot.*

For example, on the left in Figure 2-3 you see what's called a low-angle shot that's shot from below the eyeline. This is often what you see when you conference from a notebook webcam without adjusting its height. The shot on the right is shot at eye level, like the shot in Figure 2-2.

Aesthetically, the shot on the left has several problems. Because it's shot from below, my head is tilted downwards. The fluorescent lights on the ceiling convince the webcam's automatic exposure that the image is too light, so the webcam compensates by darkening the entire frame, which makes the face too dark. This is called backlighting.

Although you'll learn how to fix this problem in Chapter 6, the best fix is to avoid it in the first place.

Unless you're into intimidating your viewers, the shot has other issues. Here's what the Elements of Cinema website has to say (bit.ly/lo_angle1): "Low-angle shots are captured from a camera placed below the actor's eyes, looking up at them. Low angles make characters look dominant, aggressive, or ominous." Just the thing to close that sale, eh? Fortunately, there are several inexpensive or free fixes for low-angle shots.

*Figure 2-4. You don't have to spend a fortune to get the camera to eye level.*

For example, when I'm shooting a webinar from my MacPro's webcam, I prop it up to eye level with a cardboard box or two. Net cost, nada.

If you're a conferencing with your smartphone, consider a product like the ChargerCity smartphone tripod adapter (bit.ly/phone_mount), which can mount your phone on a tripod that you can adjust to the desired height. I picked up this unit for $13 at Amazon, and it works perfectly. However you get there, resolve to shoot your conferences from eye level. Let's move on to the second lesson from the President Kennedy video.

## Mind the Rule of Thirds

The rule of thirds dictates where the subject is positioned in the frame. Specifically, the rule divides the image into a tic-tac-toe board, and dictates that the subject be placed along one of the lines, not simply in the middle of the frame. If you scan back to the shot of President Kennedy (Figure 2-2), you'll see that his eyes are along the top vertical line and that he's positioned horizontally in the center of the frame. This rule-of-thirds positioning is used by virtually every news, sports or talk show on TV or the Internet.

That means if you don't follow the rule of thirds, as I don't do on the left in Figure 2-5, your video will look subtly weird, or simply wrong, to your viewers. They won't know it violates the rule of thirds; they'll just know it doesn't look like other talking head videos they see on TV or the Internet.

*Figure 2-5. No rule of thirds on the left; proper framing on the right.*

There are some exceptions to the rule of thirds that I'll discuss in later chapters. For this section, however, when videoconferencing and directly facing the camera, you should frame yourself horizontally in the middle of the frame with your eyes along the top line of the rule of thirds grid.

## Use Classic Framing

By framing, I mean how much of the subject is in the shot and where the subject is placed in the frame. Specifically, most TV cameramen are trained to use the classic framing shown in Figure 2-6.

For example, if you look back at the President Kennedy frame in Figure 2-2, you'll see that the picture incorporates from his armpits to the top of his head, a classic medium close-up shot. The shot on the right in Figure 2-5, from the necktie point to the top of the head, is a close-up. A shot from chin to forehead is called an extreme close-up, which you'll see in a lot of dramas, but probably isn't recommended for video calls and conferencing.

Whether you're watching news, sports, or talk shows, most shots fall into one of these classic framings. So if frame differently, and cut the shot off between the waist and the armpits, it will look weird, or off, to the viewer.

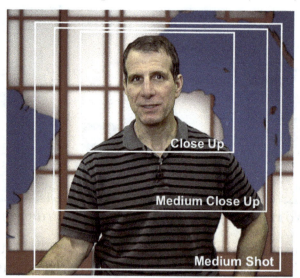

*Figure 2-6. Classic framing rules.*

If you scroll through other portions of the President Kennedy footage ([bit.ly/Pres_Kennedy](bit.ly/Pres_Kennedy)) you'll notice that the videographer used two basic shots: the close-up shown in Figure 2-2 and the medium shot shown in Figure 2-7.

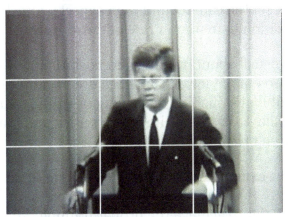

*Figure 2-7. The President in a classic medium shot.*
*(Photo courtesy National Archives.)*

Which shot should you use? That depends on how large the video is on screen. With some webinars, video can be full screen, like that shown in Figure 2-6. Here I prefer a medium shot or medium close-up. When video is in a smaller window, I prefer a medium close-up or close-up. You can see this in Figure 2-8 from a recent video interview on YouTube ([bit.ly/ROT_framing](bit.ly/ROT_framing)). Not perfect rule of thirds, but in the ballpark.

*Figure 2-8. This medium close-up works well when I'm sharing the screen with another presenter, as I am in this video.*

Actually, if you scroll though the video, you'll notice that I slouch from time to time, which drops the eyeline beneath the top third. The best advice here is to position yourself as comfortably as possible and then frame around that. Don't set the camera and then expect yourself to hold an uncomfortable position to maintain rule of thirds during the conference.

Also, don't get maniacal about framing and positioning. If you're close, that's OK for 99 percent of viewers. Just be sure to get it right before the event and be mindful of slouching or sagging or shifting during the event. Every once in a while, look at your image on screen and make sure framing and positioning aren't totally out of whack.

If you're behind the camera and filming, check if the camera has rule-of-thirds positioning guides—most prosumer and professional cameras do. This will make it easier to achieve the proper framing.

*Whether you're in front of the camera or behind it, resist the urge to make continual minor adjustments to maintain perfect framing and positioning. Most viewers will find these adjustments much more noticeable and irritating than a speaker slightly out of position.*

## Going Beyond the Webcam

Webcams are great for convenience, but they don't offer the same quality as a $400 consumer camcorder or a $4,000 prosumer model. No insult intended; it's simply a function of size and cost.

For those interested in the qualitative difference between different webcams and various camera models, check out my article in *Streaming Media Producer* entitled "Choosing Cameras and Lighting for Single-Speaker Webinars" (bit.ly/cam4webinar). I presented the same material in a webinar entitled "Choosing a Camcorder for Live Event Production" (bit.ly/cam4webinar2).

The bottom line is that as long as your lighting is good, a webcam can do a fairly credible job that's comparable to that of a $4,000 prosumer camcorder in a single-person shoot that's up close and personal. Even with good lighting, however, sometimes a webcam just won't do—for example, if your subject is presenting from a podium, or when your webinar involves a two-person interview.

In these cases, your ability to use an external camcorder depends upon your conferencing or webinar application. In all cases, you'll need to connect the camera to your computer, typically via a video capture card like the Blackmagic Design DeckLink HD Extreme I have installed on my Mac Pro (see Figure 2-9). Once installed, the software you're using has to recognize devices other than a webcam, which not all conferencing programs do.

For example, in Figure 2-9, I'm choosing the DeckLink within Google Hangouts, which lets Google Hangouts access any camera attached to the capture card. I checked on my Mac, and Skype and FaceTime enable similar access. However, some conferencing applications can only connect to a webcam and may not recognize capture cards. There's a good discussion of these issues in an article by Brent Ozar (no relation) entitled "Using an HD Camcorder as a Mac Webcam" (bit.ly/HDCAM_MacWebcam).

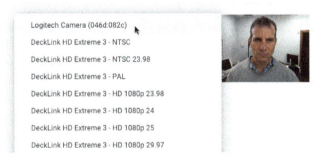

*Figure 2-9. Choosing the DeckLink from within a Google Hangout.*

In these cases, the only option is to use a device that looks like a webcam to the capture station. For example, Roland sells a series of inexpensive video mixers like the VR-50HD (bit.ly/Roland_VR-50HD) that can accept the input from up to four cameras, and outputs a webcam-compatible signal via a USB port. Connect the port to your capture station with a USB cable, and the conferencing software will treat it like input from a webcam.

It's a touch of overkill, but if you already own a unit like the Roland VR-50HD, or need one for other production purposes, it's a pretty cool solution.

## Key Takeaways

Overall, if you mind these three lessons, you'll see an instant jump in the quality of your videoconferencing and webinar productions:

> • Shoot from eye level so the webcam is pointing directly at your eyes. Don't shoot with the camera pointing upwards or downwards.

> • Adhere to the rule of thirds. Mostly this means positioning yourself in the middle of the frame with your eyes about one-third the way down the frame.

> • Use classic framing. Use a medium shot or medium close-up if the video is full screen, and a medium close-up or close-up if you're in a smaller window.

# Chapter 3: Choosing Your Background

*Figure 3-1. Two basic approaches: solid wall or open background.*

Your choice of video background can dramatically affect quality. As you'll learn in this chapter, I found that out the hard way. Fortunately, you won't have to.

There are two basic approaches to backgrounds, both shown in Figure 3-1. One is to park in front of a plain wall, as shown on the left; the other is to use a more open background. Both can work well, if you follow the rules explored in this chapter.

# Overview

Here are the background-related rules you will learn in this chapter:

- Why contrast is the most important consideration

- What contrast ratio is and why you care

- What backlighting is and how to avoid it

- How and why excessive detail and motion can degrade video quality.

Let's jump in.

## Think Contrast First

The most important function of the background is to provide good contrast with the subject—an epic fail in both videos shown in Figure 3-2. Obviously, contrast relates to both background and clothing, and sometimes hair or skin color.

*Figure 3-2. Contrast is a problem with both of these shots.*

When planning a shoot, identify the primary background color and choose clothing that contrasts well with that color. If you're producing an event, tell your speakers what colors to wear a few days in advance. For reasons explained below, it's best to avoid black suits and white shirts. Light grays, blues and browns all work much better.

If your subject's coat blends in with the background, ask them to remove the coat; perhaps their shirt will provide better contrast. If you've got a contrast problem you can't solve by adjusting clothing or background, shine a light down on the subject's hair and shoulders, as the glow will help separate them from the background.

*tip* *If you're creating an in-house set for videoconferencing, the most common background color used in broadcast is blue—the lighter the better. As you'll learn in the next section, the darker the blue, the harder it is to achieve a usable contrast ratio.*

## Minimize the Contrast Ratio

The term contrast ratio refers to the range of brightness in a frame. A frame with bright whites and dark blacks has a high contrast ratio, while a frame with muted browns and blues has a low contrast ratio. When choosing background and clothing, minimize the contrast ratio as we'll explore in Figure 3-3.

*Figure 3-3. Too much contrast ratio on the left; perfect on the right.*

The figure shows the same speaker at the same location in both shots. The framing and lighting of both shots is very similar, and the face is well exposed in both. However, because the subject is wearing a very dark red shirt on the left, the contrast ratio is much higher, which stresses out the webcam. As a result, the shirt looks like a big dark blob. On the right, where the subject is wearing brighter clothing, the contrast ratio is lower, and detail is crisp throughout the entire frame.

Why? Briefly, when your scenes have a high contrast ratio, it's hard for the camera to preserve detail at both ends of the brightness spectrum. Inexpensive cameras and high compression exacerbate the problem.

Contrast-ratio-related alarm bells should start to ring when:

- You have a black or white background

- You have a very bright light in the background

- Your subject wears high-contrast clothing, like a black suit and white shirt.

As shown on the right in Figure 3-3, it's hard to go wrong with either contrast or contrast ratio when wearing a nice brown coat and light blue shirt. It may not be the ultimate power suit, but the end result will look a whole lot better than black on white.

### Working with People of Color

Skin tones matter when it comes to contrast ratio. A few years ago, it was always fun watching golf tournaments when Vijay Singh was leading. He has very dark skin and his major sponsor, Cleveland, uses white shirts and white hats. You could almost see the frustrated camera person struggle to find an exposure setting that preserved detail in Singh's face without totally blowing out (losing detail) in the hat and shirt. Although Tiger Woods also frequently wore white hats and shirts, because his skin tone is lighter, the contrast ratio was reduced and this wasn't a problem.

If you (or your subjects) are extremely dark, avoid white clothing or backgrounds, because it will be tough to retain detail in the face without blowing out the whites.

## Police the Background

Figure 3-4 looks like a joke, but it's actually one of the strongest impetuses for me to write this book. True story. I moderated a webinar last summer during which, among other issues, both participants used white boards with lots of writing as backgrounds. While the details weren't as blatant as bank and investment passwords, at best the text was distracting, at worst, it might have communicated information best kept private. And while obviously *you* would never do anything this silly, it got me thinking that a book about producing webinars might have some value. So here we are.

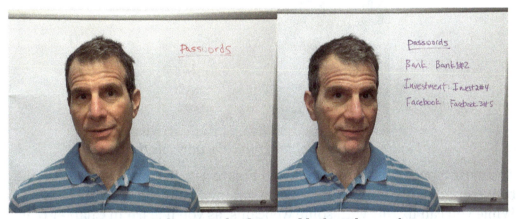

*Figure 3-4. Police your background before the conference.*

Anyway, before you start any webinar or conference, look carefully into the webcam preview window to see what's there besides your shining face. If your office is in the background, as it often is for me, it's likely that there are breakfast dishes, coffee cups, tissue boxes, water bottles, a planner, and piles of paper and other detritus in the camera view. I remove or straighten all this up before the webinar because it makes a better impression and eliminates a potential distraction.

## Avoid Backlighting

You'll learn about lighting in Chapter 5, but for now, make sure there are no bright lights in your background, since these can cause multiple problems.

*Figure 3-5. Backlighting typically darkens the face.*

The most typical problem is shown in Figure 3-5. Because there's a bright background in the frame, the webcam automatically darkens the face. While you can fix this with some webcams, as you'll learn in Chapter 6, it's best to avoid the problem altogether.

There are multiple potential issues if the bright background light is from a window. First, a dark cloud could block the sun, reducing the lighting. Second, you could have a color temperature mismatch with your indoor lighting that will cause color distortion. So it's best to avoid a window in the background for multiple reasons. More on this in Chapter 5.

Finally, bright lights can cause contrast-ratio-related issues. Overall, if you have bright lights in the background from any source, alarm bells should start to ring in your head.

## Avoid Fine Detail and Motion

Video compression is a zero-sum game; you have a fixed data rate for your video, and with most videoconferencing and webinar applications, that data rate is limited. If you have lots of fine detail in the frame, a good portion of that data must be allocated to preserve that detail, leaving less for the face, which is typically the critical element. The effect is exacerbated when the background detail is moving, as with blowing trees, shrubs or other plants.

*tip* *The term "data rate," which is defined in Chapter 1, means the amount of data per second of the compressed stream produced by your webcam.*

You can see this in Figure 3-6, which was shot against a rattan curtain, among the world's worst backgrounds. On the left, the camera preserved the detail with no problem; on the right, after compression, it's a mess.

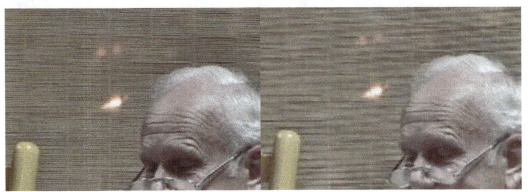

*Figure 3-6. Too much detail equals ugly video.*

Detail-related alarm bells should start to ring when:

> • You're shooting against wallpaper with intricate patterns, including company logos and text.

> • The background includes plants or other objects with fine detail, like Venetian blinds or bookshelves like those in Figure 3-3.

> • The subject is wearing fine patterns, like herringbones or tweeds. We'll see more of this in the next chapter.

## Avoid Wide-Open Spaces

Though the plain beige background worked well in Figure 3-1, and I use light blue for many live shoots, I've seen plain backgrounds blow up on several occasions, including my first ever video shoot shown on the right in Figure 3-7. I took two key lessons from the experience.

First, avoid wide-open spaces, since it gives compression technologies room to create obvious problems. I've noticed this more on reflective surfaces, and with grayish backgrounds, rather than blue, white or black. I love what the set designer did with the background on the left in Figure 3-7, since the panels and wooden widget thingies break up the background into multiple smaller areas where artifacts like banding would be much less noticeable.

*Figure 3-7. Embrace clutter, like the background on the left.*

Any time you shoot against a solid wall, banding and other unsightly artifacts should be a concern, though less so when the webcam is tightly framed on the subject, as it is on the left in Figure 3-1. That's because there's just not a lot of open space left.

> *Banding refers to the bands of grouped colors you see in the background on the right in Figure 3-7. This is caused by pixels grouping together after compression, and is exacerbated by using graduated lighting on a plain background. This occurs most often on reflective and gray backgrounds.*

The second lesson I learned is that you never really know how any background is going to work until you actually test it. If you have an important webinar or videoconference coming up, you should test your new background beforehand to avoid embarrassing problems on game day.

## Choosing the Best Background

If you take a quick look back at Figure 3-1, you'll note that it captures the two extremes of background selection. On the left is a shot against a close-in wall, while on the right is a shot with a more open background. Which is better? There are multiple considerations.

First for me is ease of use. If you're videoconferencing or producing webinars two or three times a month, you're going to need a setup that takes only a moment or two to get ready. That's the primary reason I use the setup on the right. I use standing desk, so the webcam is always eye level and ready to go. The background isn't ideal, but it's not terrible either, and it's quick and easy. It's also humanizing, as it shows me in my natural environment as opposed to against a sterile blank wall.

Second is lighting. As you'll learn in Chapter 5, I absolutely hate shadows in all my shoots, whether videoconference, webinar or for on-demand video. So if I shoot against a solid wall and need to light from the front, which I recommend, I have to deploy more lights to eliminate the shadows, adding about 20 minutes to setup time. If I'm 15 feet from the wall, shadows aren't a problem because they're so diffused.

If you don't have a convenient workspace you can use au natural, I recommend the solid wall approach. Just be sure to factor in the time necessary to get the lighting right.

# Key Takeaways

• When choosing a background, think contrast first; make sure the subject is wearing clothes that don't blend into the background.

• Mind the contrast ratio in the frame. Be concerned if there are both very bright brights and very dark darks, as detail will likely be lost in one or both of those regions.

• Avoid bright lights in the background, as this may darken the face and cause other problems. Using a window as a background is almost always a bad idea.

• Avoid fine detail or motion. Be concerned if your background has fine patterns, details, or motion—particularly if it involves small items like leaves or other plant life.

• Be concerned about wide-open backgrounds, which can cause artifacts like banding.

• Blue seems to be the most popular color for TV backgrounds, though most are too dark for my tastes.

• Test all prospective backgrounds before game day to make sure they won't cause any noticeable artifacts or other problems. There is no way to know if your background will work or not without testing.

# Chapter 4: Dressing for Success

*Figure 4-1. Perhaps a blue pinstriped shirt isn't the best idea.*

Your parents told you forever ago that you have to dress for success. Without debating the veracity of that statement for life in general, it is undoubtedly true when it comes to videoconferencing. And as you can see in Figure 4-1, the rules are quite different.

In this chapter, you will learn the webcam-related rules for dressing for success. As for the general business rules, well, you're on your own.

# Overview

Here's what you will learn in this chapter:

- What contrast ratio is and why you care (a refresher)

- Why you want to avoid excessive detail (in the unlikely event that Figure 4-1 didn't make that point strongly enough)

- Why glasses are a red flag

- How and why you need to plan for a lavalier mic hookup

- How to optimize presentation slides for use in a webinar.

## Mind the Contrast and Contrast Ratio

This is a short chapter, in part because you learned the first two key lessons on contrast and contrast ratio in Chapter 3. Briefly, when choosing colors to wear, make sure they contrast well with the background (Figure 3-2) and don't stress the contrast ratio of the webcam (Figure 3-3). This is an important point, so I'll invest another figure in the conversation.

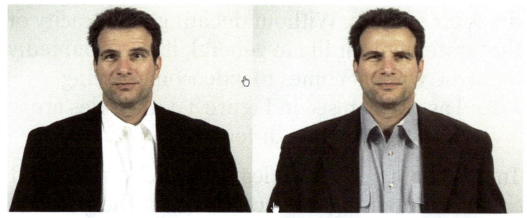

*Figure 4-2. Too much contrast ratio on the left, just right on the right.*

Figure 4-2 shows two shots produced under identical conditions. On the left, because of the extreme brightness difference between the white shirt and the black coat, detail is lost in both and the coat looks like a big blob.

The contrast ratio is simply too extreme for the camera. On the right, because the brightness difference between the blue shirt and brown coat is much less, detail is preserved in both.

The bottom line? Avoid very dark colors like blacks and dark blues, particularly if you're wearing a white shirt, and advise those you're shooting to do the same. Browns, light grays and blues do a much better job.

## Minimize Detail

We talked about minimizing detail in the last chapter, and at the start of this chapter. I'll present Figure 4-3 as an object lesson about what can happen when you don't.

*Figure 4-3. The right way and the wrong way.*

On the right is a severe example of how compression can distort clothing with excessive detail. Not only is the shirt mangled, the moire pattern is obvious and distracting. In general, fine pinstripes, herringbones and paisley patterns should be avoided at all costs—particularly when shooting with a webcam. Larger patterns, like the shirt I'm wearing on the right in Figure 4-5 are generally OK, but avoid fine patterns.

On the left, the subject is wearing the perfect outfit for live streaming: a solid sweater of one color, and a solid shirt of another color. If, for some reason, the sweater didn't contrast with the background, he could take it off, and the shirt almost certainly would. Both the sweater and the shirt are darkish, but not too dark, and won't strain the contrast ratio of the frame.

Although reddish, the sweater is a low saturated red, not a bright red that might "bloom" when encoded. Avoid neon reds, blues, greens and yellows for these reasons.

## Glasses Are a Red Flag

Glasses are a red flag because they often reflect light, particularly when located directly behind the camera. In Figure 4-4, you see what can go wrong when you're wearing glasses. To be honest, I don't wear glasses when on camera because I'm as vain as a schoolgirl, but it's obvious that glasses also complicate lighting.

*Figure 4-4. Why glasses are a red flag.*

In general, if you can go without the glasses or wear contacts during the webcam event, it greatly simplifies lighting setup. If you can't, then be sure to budget some extra time to light from the sides and avoid the reflections shown in Figure 4-4.

## Plan for Your Lavalier Microphone

If you will use a lavalier mic during your shoot, additional planning is necessary. You can see why on the left in Figure 4-5. While a casual look is great, sagging clothing is never attractive—especially when it reveals chest hair—and the modest weight of the mic is pulling it too far from the mouth. On the right, the button-down collar holds the mic without sagging.

*Figure 4-5. If you're using a lavalier mic, button-down collars are better.*

As you'll learn more about in Chapter 8, the figure on the right also shows the optimal positioning of the lavalier mic, which is about 8 inches from the chin. If the speaker is wearing a crew-neck shirt, that's difficult to achieve. So if you'll be using a lavalier mic, ask your speakers to wear a button-down shirt, or a coat for you to attach the mic to.

## Dressing Your Slides for Success

Here are some quick tips regarding slides used in webinars:

- Most webinar systems still use 4:3 aspect ratios, so check before going 16:9.

- Use sans-serif fonts, which are easier to read, with font size above 24 points, including data within tables.

- Check with your webinar provider before using large pictures or elaborate patterns, which may look degraded and can delay slide appearance.

- Check with your webinar provider before using animations and slide transitions, which many webinar systems will strip out.

- Include contact info on first and last slides.

- Offer a downloadable version whenever possible.

- Use light background and dark text; the reverse uses too much toner when printed.

# Key Takeaways

Here's a summary of items to consider when dressing for a webcam presentation (or advising your subjects how to dress).

- Does your clothing contrast well with the background (and have you told the subjects what colors to wear)?

- Are the subject's clothes either very dark or very bright, which might stress the contrast ratio of the frame?

- Is the subject wearing bright, highly saturated colors like neon reds, oranges or yellows (bad idea)?

- Do the clothes contain too much detail (pinstripes, herringbones, tweeds, paisleys)?

- Is the subject's hair neatly pulled back and otherwise not frizzing around?

- Does the subject have glasses on? If so, are they absolutely necessary? If so, you might have to light from the sides to avoid lights reflected in the glasses.

- Is the subject wearing dangling jewelry that might glitter in the light, or otherwise prove distracting?

- Are you wearing a button-down shirt that can support a lavalier mic?

# Sample Letter to Participant

Here's a letter you can send to guests who will be participating in a webcam presentation. You can download a Word version of this document at www.thewebcambook.com.

Dear: _____

Thanks for agreeing to appear on our program. Since we are shooting with a webcam, we have to take special precautions to ensure a high-quality result. Here are some recommendations to guide your on-camera appearance.

1. Solid colors are best. Please don't wear a pinstriped shirt or suit, or any kind of intricate pattern like plaid or herringbone.

2. Regarding colors *(pick one approach to include in your letter)*:

> a. The primary color in our studio background is _____. Please avoid wearing a _____ shirt or suit, with _____ or _____ being preferred choices.

> b. We're not sure which color background we'll be shooting against, so we'll need some flexibility. If possible, please wear both a solid colored shirt and coat so we can experiment to see which works best. For example, a light blue shirt and gray coat would work well, or a gray shirt and navy blue coat.

> c. Muted colors are best. Light grays, light blues and browns are best. Avoid bright reds, yellows and greens.

3. Range of colors. Please avoid an outfit with both very dark and very light colors, like a black coat and white shirt. Darker colors often lose detail and end up looking like blobs. Again, browns, light blues and light grays tend to work best.

4. Button-down shirts are preferred. We will be attaching a lavalier mic to your shirt, so a button-down shirt will allow for ideal placement and support.

5. Grooming. Neatly groomed hair works best for webcam presentations. Please comb hair neatly or pull hair back.

6. Please limit the jewelry that you wear. In particular, leave off chains, hoop earrings and similar dangling items. Muted items like pearls or dark stones are definitely preferred, although less is more.

7. If you can do without your glasses, please do. Otherwise, we'll light around them.

That's it. Thanks again for agreeing to appear on our program.

# Chapter 5: Simple Lighting Techniques

*Figure 5-1. My $30 solution for lighting webcam-based productions.*

The cheaper the camera, the more you need extra lights to optimize quality. Since webcams are as cheap as cameras get, you should never produce a webinar or videoconference without some extra lighting. You don't need to spend a fortune; as Figure 5-1 shows, $30 will do. But you should consider adding some lights whenever possible.

In this chapter, you'll learn what to look for when buying extra lights, and how to use them once you've got them.

# Overview

Here's what you'll learn in this chapter:

- Why lighting is so important to video quality

- The philosophy of lighting for webcam productions

- Lighting fundamentals like color temperature and hard versus soft lights

- The various types of lights you can buy, including clamp lights, compact fluorescent soft boxes, and LED lights

- How to avoid shadows in the background (assuming you feel as strongly about shadows as I do) and other lighting techniques.

Let's jump right in.

# Why Lighting is Key

Many webcam-based videos are produced solely with ambient lighting, which typically means overhead fluorescent lights. This causes multiple issues that reduce the quality of your video, some of which are obvious in the frame on the left in Figure 5-2.

To explain, the frame on the left is shot solely with overhead lights, while I added lights for the shot on the right. On the left, while the forehead is well lit, the bottom of the face is clearly too dark. Although it's not obvious in the screen shot, the frame on the left is grainier, which is caused by the webcam boosting brightness to compensate for inadequate lighting. As I'll discuss in the next section, a major goal when lighting your webcam production is to make the scene bright enough so that your webcam doesn't have to boost it further.

*Figure 5-2. On the left, shot solely with overhead lighting; on the right, webcam with supplemental lights. Yeah, I know, the sweater is too dark.*

Beyond the graininess, on the right, the facial colors look more natural, the face is shadow free, and the wrinkles on my forehead much less noticeable. All this from about $200 in lighting gear and 20 minutes of setup time, both clearly worth it if your webinar or videoconference is mission critical.

## Lighting for Webcam Goals

Let's discuss the goal of lighting for webcam productions and how this differs from lighting for traditional productions. When lighting for traditional video productions, more light is usually better. If the lights are too bright, you can clamp down the camcorder's aperture and make it work. But it's almost impossible for the lights to be too bright.

Webcam lighting is different. If the lights are too bright, you can overwhelm the webcam, which usually don't have the same mechanical aperture control as much larger camcorders. Your goal should be to project just enough light on the subject to eliminate graininess in the video, and to eliminate shadows from the background, if shadows are a problem.

While you can set up your lights without the subject, you should make the final intensity-related adjustments with the subject in place and the webcam running. I know it's a pain where you're producing a selfie (believe me, I know), but there's no other way.

Finally, setting up lights and controlling exposure, which you'll learn about next chapter, go hand in hand. You really can't do one effectively without knowing how to do the other.

I'm not trying to make this sound complicated; 90 percent of the time you can get by with a clamp light and automatic exposure settings. But the remaining 10 percent of the time, particularly if you're shooting in a dark environment, you'll have to be proficient with lighting and setting exposure to produce adequate visual quality. And there are very few productions that can't benefit from extra lights and a bit of exposure tweaking.

# Lighting Fundamentals

Let's start with a few fundamentals you need to know about before you can buy and use lights and light kits.

## All Lights Have Different Color Temperatures

Most definitions of color temperature are so complex that they have little utility to webcam practitioners. For example, Wikipedia states, "The color temperature of a light source is the temperature of an ideal black-body radiator that radiates light of comparable hue to that of the light source." That clear it up for you?

Here's my attempt. You're probably aware that candles and old light bulbs are a bit yellowish in color, while fluorescent lights can be bluish. Imagine holding a white board up to each type of light. In my definition, color temperature is the tinge this white board assumes from each light.

The relevant scale is called Kelvin, or K. Kelvin values from 1700 to 3500 K turn your white board orange or yellow, and are typically referred to as incandescent. Lights ranging from 5000 to 6500 K turn your whiteboard slightly bluish, and are called daylight or fluorescent—although you have be careful because some fluorescent bulbs have a color temperature in the 3200 K range. It's critical that all lights have different color temperatures, and unless you match them closely, bizarre things can happen.

### Flashpoint 500C LED Light

**Key Features**

- **50%-5900 K (Kelvin) Color Temperature**
- **50%-3200 K (Kelvin) Color Temperature**

*Figure 5-3. The two most widely used color temperatures.*

When choosing a light, there are generally two alternatives: around 5900 K for fluorescent lights, and 3200 K for incandescent and some fluorescent lights. Most lights are one temperature or the other, but as shown in Figure 5-3, some offer both for greater flexibility. Both temperatures work equally well, since most webcams will automatically white-balance the shot to produce the proper color and make white look like white. Problems occur when you mix both color temperatures in the same shot, because the webcam can't correct this. You can see this in Figure 5-4.

*Figure 5-4. Daylight in back and incandescent lights up front make for an impossible white balance adjustment.*

In the shot, there's an incandescent light in front, which has a color temperature of 3200 K, and daylight in the back, with a color temperature of around 5900 K. On the right, the white balance is set to 3200 K, which makes the white shirt look white but the light streaming in from outside look blue. On the left, the white balance is set to 5900 K, which makes the outdoor light look natural but the shirt and skin look yellow.

Obviously, if you had to choose between the two, you'd go with the shot on the right. However, if both lights were on the subject's front, both white balance settings would cause some color distortion. For example, if your overhead fluorescent lights were 5900 K and you supplemented them with 3200 K incandescent lights, you could have a disaster.

For this reason, when buying and deploying lights, it's critical to ensure that their color temperatures match other lights you'll be using. In my office, the overhead fluorescent lights are 5900 K bulbs, the compact fluorescent bulbs I use are 5900 K, and the LCD panels are 5900 K, so I can mix and match as needed. I can also let the light stream in from my windows during most daylight hours without worrying about a conflict.

If you need to match both daylight and incandescent lighting, you can buy a dual-color light like the Adorama Flashpoint 500C shown in Figure 5-3, or place a transparent sheet called a gel over the light to convert the color temperature (Figure 5-9).

### Grokking White Balancing

A few pages ago, I described color temperature as the color that a light projects onto a theoretical white board placed near the light. When you white-balance a webcam, you tell it which color that is.

Here's what I mean. When you manually white-balance a camcorder, you point it at a white object and press the white-balance button. Essentially you're telling the camcorder, "hey, this is white." The camera analyzes the white object, detects the color temperature of the lighting, and adjusts all colors accordingly.

With auto white balance, which most webcams use, the device attempts to detect the lighting's color temperature and adjust it automatically. Obviously, this works better in some instances than in others. Fortunately, some webcams let you adjust white balance manually if there are problems, as you will learn in Chapter 6.

## Hard versus Soft Lights

Hard lights are typically incandescent bulbs that create copious amounts of harsh light with hard shadows, as shown on the left in Figure 5-5. Soft lights have a more diffused quality that produces less defined shadows, and are the preferred light source for webcam and other streaming shoots. However, soft lights are less intense than hard lights, so you'll typically need more or larger bulbs to create the same power as a hard light.

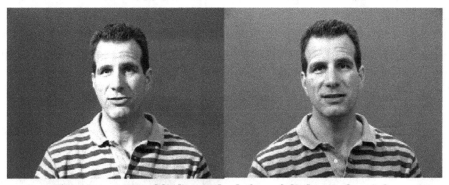

*Figure 5-5. Hard light on the left, soft light on the right.*

Ten years ago, most light fixtures used tungsten or incandescent bulbs that produced hard light, so you had to diffuse the light by bouncing it off an umbrella or ceiling. Hard lights also ran very hot and drew lots of power, making them hard to work with—particularly in offices and other closed spaces. Most hard lights are 3200 K, making them tough to use with office fluorescent lights, or with daylight streaming in from open windows.

Fortunately, the most common light sources available today are compact fluorescent (CFL) and LED lights that produce soft light, and also draw less power and generate less heat than hard lights. But if you borrow a light from your A/V department (assuming you have an A/V department), they just might hand you an older incandescent fixture that produces an unsuitably hard light—not to mention raises your office temperature by 15 degrees. Also, if you're considering screwing a 100-watt incandescent bulb into a clamp light, you should know that the hard light it produces won't be particularly flattering and probably will cause white-balance-related issues if used in conjunction with fluorescent lights.

# Inexpensive Lights and Light Kits

With this as background, let's take a closer look at the types of lights you should consider for use with your webcam.

## Clamp Lights

When I'm conferencing or producing a webinar at my standing desk, my go-to lighting instrument is a clamp light configured with a daylight balanced 15-watt bulb. I keep the overhead fluorescent lights on and the windows unblocked, and the clamp light delivers enough power to light the bottom of my face (Figure 5-6). Total cost of the setup? Less than $30.

*Figure 5-6. This light delivers enough power to light the bottom of my face.*

This setup works because I'm far enough away from the back wall that shadows aren't an issue. I can either hang the clamp light on another computer monitor or clamp it on a window frame, and at 15 watts, the light doesn't cause any deer-in-the-headlights look, even though it's pretty close to my face.

Overall it's a cheap, effective system I use for 85 percent of my webcam productions. The other 15 percent, when I shoot against a blue back wall in my office, requires another solution that's a touch more expensive and complicated and involves the use of a different class of lighting implement.

*tip* *The best way to assess your lighting setup is to record some video and look that over, rather than try to gauge the results in real time. Most webcam software apps have recording capabilities, so this should be simple to do.*

## Compact Fluorescent Soft Boxes

Compact fluorescent (CFL) soft boxes were the first affordable kits that delivered soft lighting for webcam and streaming producers. In many ways, they are the ideal light; most come with color temperatures that match overhead fluorescent bulbs, they're cool so you can place them very near the subject, and they don't draw much power, so you can deploy them without worrying about blowing a fuse or maxing out the air conditioner. Figure 5-7 shows a pair of soft boxes used to light a webcam-based webinar.

*Figure 5-7. A pair of CFL soft boxes light this webcam-based webinar.*

You can buy lights like these for about $70 apiece, usually in three- or four-light kits; I have five soft boxes total that I use quite frequently. While they're essential to my productions, there are several reasons I probably won't buy any more.

First, the lights are big and bulky, which makes them a pain to store and use at times. Second, there's no easy way to target or shape the light, which can make them hard to use in some instances, which you'll see below.

Although it's not an issue for me, these lights don't travel well; they take 10 to 15 minutes per light to assemble and aren't that robust, so you don't get the sense they'll last that long if you repeatedly disassemble and reassemble them. I keep mine fully assembled and in a storeroom, so they've worked out well for me.

If you're considering buying a CFL soft box, you should ignore the wattage equivalency claims and focus on the number of bulbs in the unit. Most have either four or five ~45-watt bulbs, and should work well to about 8 feet from the subject. Make sure the light is dimmable; the best units let you turn each light on or off separately. Buy from a vendor with user reviews and read them before choosing your gear.

## LED Lights

LED lights are the newest soft light, and as far as I'm concerned, all I'll ever buy going forward, although they cost more than CFL soft boxes. Why so bullish? Because they provide slightly stronger light than CFLs while eliminating the major negatives.

Consider the Adorama Flashpoint CL-1300 shown in Figure 5-8. It's only 2 inches thick, so you can place it almost anywhere, and it comes with a travel bag, so it's highly portable and fast and easy to set up and take down. The barn door option on the unit (those black hingey looking things on all four sides) lets you shape the light, so it's easier to deploy than a soft box. As of early 2015, you can buy the unit for around $360 with barn doors— although it a lacks a light pole, which will set you back another $50 to $80.

Note that this is a 1000 bulb unit, which is roughly twice as powerful as the four- or five-bulb CFL light kits shown in Figure 5-7. I really liked the CL-1300, and you can read my review at bit.ly/CL_1300.

*Figure 5-8. The Adorama Flashpoint CL-1300, a great LED panel.*

Note that there are 500-bulb LED lights that deliver about the same power as typical CFL softboxes, and cost around $150. Some first-generation LED panels had quality-control issues, so be sure to read reviews before buying a unit, and buy from a reputable vendor with a reasonable return policy. You can read my review of the FlashPoint 500C LED light shown in Figure 5-3 at bit.ly/LED_lights.

*Figure 5-9. The CL-1300 comes with a 3200 K gel and diffuser.*

There are several other features to consider when buying an LED panel. Most are dimmable, so that shouldn't be an issue. However, if you'll be mixing the LED lighting with existing incandescent lighting, you'll need a 3200 K gel, which is the darker panel shown at the top of Figure 5-9. As you probably guessed, the gel converts the bluish light produced by the LED bulbs into yellowish light that matches incandescent lights.

Also, although it's not a problem that I've noticed, some shooters claim that the individual bulbs in an LED panel can cause "multiple shadow effect," which is why Adorama includes the diffusion filter also shown in Figure 5-9. Finally, note that you can buy LED panels in both incandescent and fluorescent color values, so make sure you're getting the desired color value before you make your final click.

> *Once you go beyond a simple clamp light, the time required to set up and fine-tune lighting can skyrocket—particularly for selfie webinars and videoconferences. Optimizing lighting is critical for quality and definitely worth it, but be sure to budget the necessary time, particularly the first time you use a new lighting setup.*

# Simple Lighting Techniques

Before you go shopping for lights, you should learn about common lighting techniques that you'll probably use in your conferencing or webcam events. Whole books have been written about this stuff; I'll just cover those critical to videoconferencing.

## Avoiding Shadows

When you're shooting close to a solid background, shadows become an issue. Maybe it's just me, but I find shadows distracting and a sign of poor lighting skills or lack of attention. Perhaps it's because any time I see a shadow, it reminds me of the video shown in Figure 5-10. I wasn't in charge of this production, didn't pay attention to the lighting, and was less than pleased with the results.

*Figure 5-10. Me and my (gulp) shadow.*

Whenever I shoot against a wall, if shadows are a problem, I deploy four lights, roughly as shown in Figure 5-11. The two back lights shining against the wall are roughly at the level of my head, while the two lights in front are about 20 percent higher than my head, pointing down. You can see how barn doors would come in handy for the backlights, since it's tough to keep the light from spilling on to the subject as well as the background.

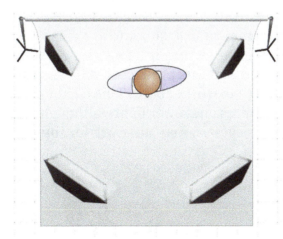

*Figure 5-11. Light placement when shooting close against a wall.*

Figure 5-12 shows a picture of the actual event using this setup, with the resultant shadow-free video on the right. It takes about 15 minutes to get the lighting set up, but when I'm really trying for top production quality, it's worth the time and effort.

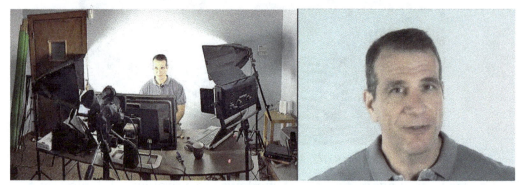

*Figure 5-12. Here's the actual setup and resultant shadow-free frame.*

You can see that three of the four lights are CFL soft boxes, augmented by an LED light panel to my front left. Technically, the two lights in front are called key lights, since they're of equal intensity because I wanted to avoid shadows on my face. This is called flat lighting and it's the technique I recommend for webinars and other live events.

Another lighting arrangement is to shoot with a single LED light behind the webcam lighting the face, which is how I shot both frames in Figure 5-13. On the left, you see that this produces a slight shadow behind my head, which isn't enough to worry about. This technique is called single-key lighting, and it requires one fewer light—although that light is directly shining in the speaker's eyes, so may not work for some presenters.

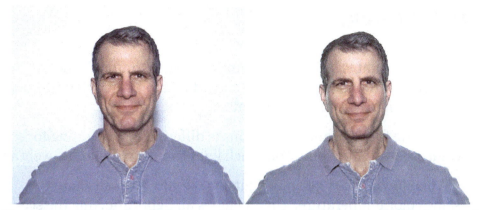

*Figure 5-13. Single key lighting, without and with lights on the background.*

If you look closely at the frame on the left in Figure 5-13, you'll notice tiny imperfections in the wall. I can make the shadow and the imperfections go away by lighting the background as shown in Figures 5-11 and 5-12, the results of which you can see on the right in Figure 5-13. This brightens the background considerably, which adds to the contrast and is my go-to lighting setup for important conferences and webinars.

*(!) (tip) Unless you're in your 20s and have a body fat percentage in the single digits, close-up shots of your neckline may not be flattering. By positioning the lights and camera slightly above the subject, you can hide the neck in the shadows, producing a flattering chin line like that shown in Figure 5-13 (if I do say so myself).*

# Key Takeaways

• Ambient light is seldom sufficient to produce optimal results without additional lighting. You should plan on deploying additional lights for all webcam-based events.

• Lighting for webcam productions is different from lighting for camcorder productions. Too much light can overwhelm the webcam.

• When buying or deploying lights, make sure they all share the same color temperature. That includes all lights affecting the scene, including overhead lights and daylight streaming in the window.

• Soft lights are preferable to hard lights for multiple reasons, including softer shadows, less power and less heat.

• If you're not shooting against a wall or shadows aren't objectionable to you, a $10 clamp light with a $20 CFL bulb may be all you need.

• CFL soft boxes are inexpensive, but they don't travel well and are bulky, and the light is hard to control.

• LED panels deliver slightly stronger light than CFL soft boxes. They're smaller and more portable, and they can use barn doors for light control.

• If you're shooting against a wall, shadows may be an issue. If that's the case, you can shine lights on the background to eliminate the shadows and improve the appearance of the back wall.

• You can use one or two key lights when lighting a webinar or videoconference. One key light is slightly simpler but shines the light directly in the speaker's eyes, so this setup may be more challenging for novice speakers.

# Chapter 6: Optimizing Your Webcam Settings

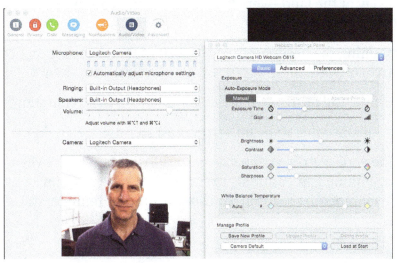

*Figure 6-1. Fine-tuning the settings on my Logitech webcam.*

When it comes to webcam-based video, the best case is when the webcam produces well-exposed and accurately colored video in full auto mode. Unfortunately, this doesn't always happen. When it doesn't, you'll have to adjust exposure and color manually, which you'll learn how to do in this chapter.

# Overview

Here are the topics covered in this chapter:

- The lay of the land—very little standardization in webcam control software, so very little consistency

- Obtaining the necessary tools—most Mac webcams don't come with control software; here you'll learn how to get your own

- Defining the terms—what I mean by luminance, color, and focus

- Optimizing your webcam settings—a step-by-step guide.

Towards the end, there's a deep dive into the differences between brightness, gamma and contrast. Definitely not necessary for most readers, but perhaps interesting reading for those who want to understand the nuts and bolts.

*This chapter comes after the chapter on lighting for a reason. You should set up your lights first to produce the optimal environment, and then fine-tune your webcam configuration if necessary. If you're unable to deploy lights for some reason, you may find yourself performing major surgery with your webcam configuration items to get the most usable video.*

# Lay of the Land

Unfortunately, there is little standardization when it comes to webcam-related luminance and color adjustments. Most Windows-based webcams offer some customization controls, but the configuration options are usually different from webcam to webcam, and program to program.

In addition, not all videoconferencing or webinar programs let you configure your webcam while they are running, and many ignore existing webcam configurations when they start the webcam, so fine-tuning your settings before launching the program has no effect.

Those caveats aside, there are many instances where configuring your webcam is possible and can improve your video quality. And there are some general principles that you can use to select the best configuration options and apply them most effectively. So that's what I'll cover in this chapter.

While most Windows webcams come with configuration software, most Mac webcams don't. So let's start with a look at the available Mac options.

## Get the Necessary Tools

Though I use a Mac every day (typing on one as we speak), I often don't subscribe to the underlying Apple policy that simple is always better. One case where I vehemently disagree is in webcam operation, where most Mac webcams do not natively include configuration options like those shown in Figure 6-1 and throughout this chapter.

Fear not; there are a couple of apps you can try. On the left in Figure 6-2 is Mactaris Webcam Settings, which I have installed on a Mac Pro, driving a Logitech HD Webcam C615 (and an iSight camera on one of my Mac monitors on another system). The program costs $7.99 and should work with all USB-based webcams, but not FireWire and other webcams. Check mactaris.blogspot.com for more information.

*Figure 6-2. Two apps that let you configure your webcam on the Mac.*

The Logitech Camera Settings app shown on the right in Figure 6-2 is free, but offers fewer features than the Webcam Settings app with no control over exposure or gain, which are critical controls. Even if you have a

Logitech webcam, try that one first. I couldn't find a compatibility list, but the program worked fine with my C615 webcam.

Note that I couldn't find an equivalent program for iOS or Android devices. It seems that if you're making the bulk of your video calls on mobile devices, you're stuck with either automatic operation (iOS) or very limited color-related adjustments (Android).

With this as background, let's start looking at how to optimize your video quality before or during a videoconference or webinar. Let's start by figuring out what it all means.

## Defining the Terms

Let's define some terms to avoid confusion down the road. When you manually control your webcam, you have three major considerations: luminance, color, and focus. By luminance, I mean the relative brightness or darkness of a video, which you might adjust with controls like exposure, gain, brightness, contrast, and gamma—sometimes all of the above.

When I say adjust luminance first, I'm not trying to use a fancy word, I'm trying to avoid confusion. If I said adjust exposure first, or brightness first, and these controls weren't available in the software you're using, it could be misleading. So I'll use luminance to describe the brightness of the video, because I've never seen a luminance adjustment in any webcam program.

By color, I mean the accuracy and intensity of the color in the video, and I typically attack this second after getting luminance under control. Sometimes, after adjusting color you might want to tweak luminance, but it's tough to adjust color when the video is too dark to see.

Finally, by focus I mean the sharpness in the video, which could involve both focus and sharpness controls. Again, the order of attack is luminance, color, and focus.

# Optimizing Your Webcam Settings

Now that we know what we're talking about, we're ready to begin optimizing your webcam settings. Here are the recommended steps.

## Step 1. Get into Your Production Setup

I recommend testing and fine-tuning your video setup one business day before the actual event. That way, all you have to do the day of is to turn on your gear and load your presets.

To configure your webcam, you'll need to be in your full production setup. This means you need to go to the location of the actual webinar or videoconference and set up any lights or other gear. If possible, you should be wearing clothing close to what you anticipate wearing for the actual event.

## Step 2. Access Your Webcam Controls

This will vary by operating system and program. If you're running a Mac and acquire the Mactaris Webcam Settings or similar program, you can access these controls anytime you're using your webcam. Just open it up like any other Mac program and you'll be able to adjust your webcam settings as shown in Figure 6-1, although program controls may change from webcam to webcam.

If you're running Windows, you'll only be able to adjust your webcam when using programs that provide access to the controls within the interface— such as Skype, as shown in Figure 6-3. Click Tools > Options and Skype will load the Options panel shown in the figure. Click Video Settings on the left-hand menu, and a button labeled Webcam Settings will appear. Click that button and your webcam adjustments will appear. Those shown in the figure are from the embedded Webcam in my HP notebook.

Other programs, like Oovoo, also provide access to these controls. Unfortunately, some browser-based apps like Google Hangouts+, don't. Unlike on the Mac, if you try to open your webcam software once the webcam is already running Google Hangouts+, you'll probably get a "No Webcam Detected" or similar message, because the webcam is running in Google Hangouts+ and can't be accessed by the webcam software. That's what happened when I tried to run the HP webcam software on my HP notebook while in a Google Hangout.

*Figure 6-3. Accessing your webcam controls from Skype.*

If you can't optimize your settings while in a videoconferencing or webinar program, try optimizing your settings before you enter the program. All webcams ship with some control software; just run the program, adjust the settings as detailed in this chapter, save the settings, and then launch the conferencing or other program. While I can't guarantee that the webcam will pick up those settings once in the conferencing program, this procedure does work with the webcam on my HP notebook.

## Step 3. Disable Auto Mode (If Necessary)

Whenever possible, I run webcam events in auto mode. Webcams have improved their ability to handle a variety of environments and lighting situations with aplomb, and when you're in a conference or a webinar, the last thing you need to worry about is luminance and color. So, I configure my webcam manually only when absolutely required.

Here are some signs you should consider going manual:

• The video is clearly too dark, too light, or the color is off

• The face is too dark

• The luminance brightens or darkens noticeably when you move around in the frame, or when other minor changes occur (For example, if a dark-haired speaker looks down, auto mode might automatically boost brightness to compensate. Or if the speaker bends down, revealing a light back wall, or lifts a piece of paper into the frame, the webcam might darken the video. These unintended adjustments are distracting and look unprofessional.)

• The video moves in and out of focus

• You have a problem with your background, like a very bright light that you can't physically correct.

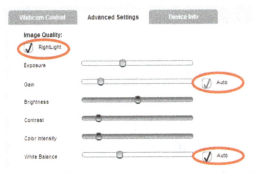

*Figure 6-4. Disabling auto operation in the Windows version of Logitech software.*

Note that many of these problems will only appear when you haven't followed the rules of background, clothing and lighting detailed in the previous chapters. If you do a good job with these fundamentals, odds are you'll be able to use auto mode with your webcam and have one less problem to worry about.

To run in manual mode, you have to disable auto mode. You'll do this in different ways with different programs, but usually there will be auto controls for both luminance and color. For example, in the Webcam

Settings screen shown in Figure 6-1, you have to choose Manual Auto-Exposure mode in the Exposure settings bar near the top, and deselect Auto in the White Balance Temperature area on the lower left. In the Logitech Windows software shown in Figure 6-4, you have to deselect the three highlighted checkboxes. You'll know you missed a box if the manual adjustments are grayed out or otherwise in accessible.

### Some Quick Definitions

I spend a good bit of time later in the chapter showing you what brightness, contrast and gamma are and how they work. Until then, here are some quick definitions.

*Brightness* adjusts the luminance value of all pixels in a frame by the same value.

*Contrast* adjusts the degree of separation between the brightest and darkest clips in a frame.

*Gamma* adjusts the image's midtone values without affecting black and white levels.

You can understand why a visual explanation is necessary to make these concepts usable. It's available in Step 6.

*You probably remember this, but adjust luminance, then color, then focus.*

## Step 4. Adjust Exposure First (If Available)

Here, I'm being literal. If exposure controls are available, adjust them first. Here's why. Exposure typically adjusts the mechanics of the webcam sensor that captures the video, while other controls—like brightness and contrast—process the video after capture. In other words, exposure controls adjust *how the video is captured* while other controls *process the video after capture*. Best practice is to process the video as minimally as possible, so when exposure controls are available, you should always use them first. In other words, they all affect perceived brightness, but the exposure control does it most efficiently.

If there is an exposure or exposure time control, first set other controls—like brightness, contrast, and gamma—at their default positions, which should be zero or the equivalent. You want them to have no impact on image brightness. Set gain to zero (I'll explain why in a moment). With most webcams, you can accomplish this by clicking a Default or Reset button.

Then use the exposure control to adjust video brightness. Understand that this control adjusts how long the webcam takes to record an image, like shutter speed on a video camera. If it takes a long time (shutter speed slow), the video is brighter, but the individual frames can blur.

*Figure 6-5. Exposure Time essentially controls shutter speed.*

You can see this in Figure 6-5. On the left, Exposure Time is about 20 percent, while Brightness and Contrast are in their default positions. The hand waving slowly in front of the camera is fairly crisp. On the right, Exposure is around 40 percent and I've adjusted Brightness to the left to compensate, though the video is slightly brighter. Because the exposure time is longer (shutter speed slower), the moving hand is blurry and indistinct.

## Step 5. Then Adjust Gain (If Available)

As long as you have a decent amount of light, you should be able to achieve sufficient brightness via the exposure control without producing any blurriness. If light is low, however, and you slow exposure time excessively, the video may become too blurry. This is the case with an iSight camera on one of my Macs; if I slow exposure time even slightly to brighten the frame, the video becomes blurry and unusable. In this case, set exposure to a level that produces a crisp image, and boost either gain or brightness/contrast to provide sufficient luminance.

When the interface provides access to both gain and brightness/contrast adjustments, which is better?

By definition, gain adjusts the sensitivity of the image sensors in the webcam, like ISO ratings in film or digital cameras. Boosting sensor sensitivity increases brightness and contrast, but it injects noise into the video, as does boosting brightness. Because gain adjusts the incoming image, not the image after it's acquired, I typically adjust gain rather than brightness/contrast.

How do you know when the image is "correct," or "optimized," or otherwise OK? Technically, there is no objective standard. Basically, try to make sure the face is bright enough for normal conversation. You'll see more on this in the sections below.

It's unlikely, though possible, that adjusting exposure and gain may not produce sufficient luminance for your videos. In addition, there may be cases where there is an exposure control but no gain control. In both cases, you'll have to adjust brightness, contrast, and perhaps gamma to produce the optimal luminance. I explain these concepts in the next section.

## Step 6. When no Exposure or Gain, Adjust Brightness/Contrast/Gamma

Some programs don't provide exposure controls, or provide exposure with no gain. This would be the case if you were presented with controls like those shown in Figure 6-6, which are the configuration options for the webcam on my HP notebook. Here you have to adjust luminance with brightness, contrast and gamma controls. What's the order of attack?

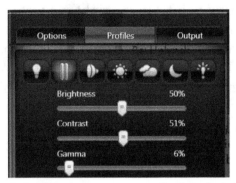

*Figure 6-6. No exposure controls; just brightness,
contrast and gamma.*

The quick and easy answer would be that you wiggle the controls around until you get an image that looks good, and then move on. A more technical answer would be:

- Adjust gamma first until the image is sufficiently bright

- Then adjust contrast to remove the dinginess from the image.

The "holy cow, what was I thinking?" answer comes now. It's a pretty deep dive into what actually happens when you adjust brightness, contrast, and gamma. It certainly isn't necessary to produce appropriate luminance values with a webcam, but it's fundamental knowledge that's useful under a range of circumstances. So read on if you'd like, or skip to the next section.

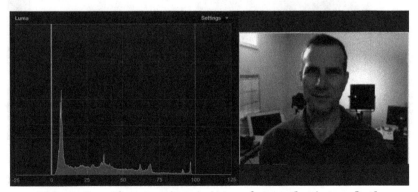

*Figure 6-7. Our starting point: a frame that's too dark.*

Figure 6-7 is our starting point. On the right is a webcam frame that's clearly too dark. On the left is a histogram that shows the distribution of pixels in the frame according to their brightness on what's called the IRE scale, for Institute of Radio Engineers (of all groups). An IRE value of 0, which is on the extreme left, represents solid black, while an IRE value of 100, on the extreme right, represents solid white. Because the video frame is so dark, the largest cluster of pixels is on the left hand side, close to black, which represents the dark purple shirt, plus the dark pixels in the monitors behind me.

For reference, if my face was well lit, the IRE value of my face would be around 70 IRE. While there are some pixels at that value, the hump isn't big enough to represent my face. So the histogram (borrowed from a video editing program called Apple Final Cut Pro X), confirms what your eyes see: the video is too dark.

In Figure 6-8, I've increased **brightness** to the max. From the histogram, you see that increasing brightness boosts the luminance of **all** pixels in the frame, moving them all to towards higher IRE values. So the clump of pixels near the 0 IRE value in Figure 6-8 is now at 50. The face is lighter, but the image looks dingy because there are no black pixels. You might say it lacks contrast, which neatly leads us into the next adjustment.

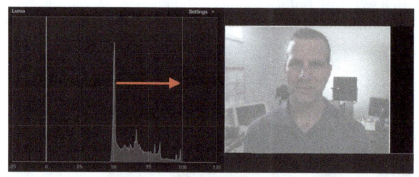

*Figure 6-8. Adjusting only brightness.*

When you boost the **contrast** in a video, which I've done in Figure 6-9, you increase the difference between the darkest and lightest pixels in the video. Like the arrow in Figure 6-9 shows, you're pushing the darker pixels to the left and the brighter pixels to the right. This returns some pixels close to their original IRE value of 0, which returns contrast to the image. It looks better, but unfortunately, the face is still too dark.

I hear you thinking, "Wouldn't it be lovely if we could brighten only the pixels in the face, and not those at the darkest and lightest extremes?" Well, when available, that's precisely what the *gamma* adjustment attempts to do. Here's the definition of gamma adjustment from the Adobe Premiere Pro (another popular video editor) help file: "Adjusts the image's midtone values without affecting black and white levels."

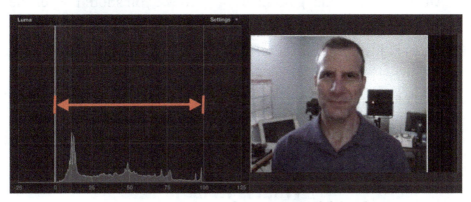

*Figure 6-9. Boosting the contrast of the video.*

As shown in Figure 6-10, gamma works primarily on the mid-range pixels (according to their luminance values), in this case making them brighter without affecting the darkest or lightest pixels in the frame. Since you don't pull the darkest pixels from their low IRE values, there's no dinginess, and this produces the best result yet.

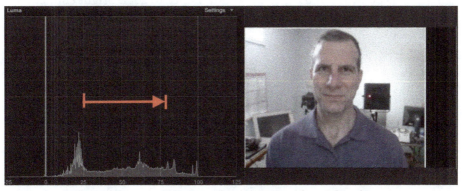

*Figure 6-10. Adjusting the gamma of a video frame.*

OK, truth time. All images are simulations to illustrate the adjustments via the now familiar histograms, although the descriptions are technically accurate. Now you know what brightness, contrast and gamma controls actually do, and how and when to best use them. Some final thoughts:

• As previously stated, when brightness and gamma are both available, try gamma first. Typically, you care most about the face, and the luminance values of the face should be in the midtones.

• Any time you adjust gamma or brightness, you should experiment with contrast to see if it improves the video.

• When adjustments get totally hosed, hit the Reset button (or the equivalent) and start over.

• If you look at the face in Figure 6-10, you can see noise around all edges. Increasing brightness via webcam controls is never free; it's almost always accompanied by noise. It's always better to add lights than to boost the brightness with webcam controls.

## What is Noise?

When I talk about noise in a video, I'm talking about visible graininess that appears when you've over-boosted luminance, or when a video is too dark. Noise is distracting to your viewers, and it makes it harder to compress the video while retaining good quality because the codec sees the noise as detail that it needs to preserve.

You can minimize noise by lighting your subject effectively. When lighting is poor, you'll have to boost luminance to get a bright enough image, or the webcam will do it automatically—which produces noise in both cases.

## Step 7. Adjust Hue and Saturation (Color)

Once you've adjusted brightness, it's time to tackle color. Again, if the color looks good to you in Auto, leave it alone; most webcams have gotten pretty good at auto white balancing.

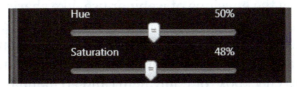

*Figure 6-11. The two most common color-related controls.*

If you must adjust color manually, there are typically two controls: hue and saturation. Hue adjustments change the actual colors in the video, you should adjust this first. The approach is simple: move the slider or turn the dial until the colors in the video look accurate.

Saturation adjusts the intensity of the color in the video. Drag the slider all the way to the left (usually) and you get black-and-white video. All the way to the right, and you go psychedelic. I usually boost saturation to add a bit of color to my face, but I'm careful not to overdo it.

*It's easy to stray down the rabbit hole when adjusting color, and often the more time you spend, the worse it looks. Less is often more when it comes to color adjustments.*

## Step 8. Adjust Focus and Sharpness

I use auto focus unless I notice the webcam losing focus during a practice session or conference, which seldom occurs. Auto-focus algorithms have improved dramatically over time, and the typical conference setup, with a close-up of the speaker directly in the middle of the frame (in rule-of-thirds positioning, of course), is not a challenging scenario for these auto controls.

*Figure 6-12. I mostly use auto focus.*

If you're stretching the envelope of webinar use, like sharing a webcam between two speakers, positioning yourself off to the side, or moving around a lot—particularly with a wall close behind you—you may notice the webcam gaining and losing focus frequently. In these instances, you should de-select the Auto checkbox (or equivalent) and go manual.

To manually focus the webcam, position yourself where you will be during the bulk of the conference, and drag the focus slider until the image is as sharp as possible. Remember that when in manual focus mode, if you move significantly closer to or away from the camera, it will lose focus; if you plan on moving around a lot, auto focus is probably a better operating mode.

Sharpness is a related option that technically increases the contrast around edges in the video, making it look sharper. I rely on focus (auto or manual) to provide realistic focus and typically don't manually add sharpness to the video. So, I leave sharpness at its default setting.

# Other Configurations

There several other common configuration options offered by webcam software programs, so let's cover these as well.

## Zoom/Pan/Tilt

Some webcams include zoom controls that let you zoom into an image, and then pan (move left or right) or tilt (move up and down) within the zoomed in frame. While I'm sure these capabilities are valuable in some applications, I've never used them in a videoconference or webinar.

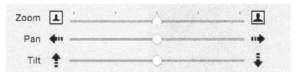

*Figure 6-13. I never use Zoom/Pan/Tilt controls in a videoconference.*

## Anti-flicker Controls

Another problem I've never run into is power-line flicker, which reportedly can manifest as dark bands running horizontally through your video. Perhaps I haven't experienced this problem because most webcam programs enable anti-flicker automatically, although even when I've disabled the function, I haven't seen the problem.

*Figure 6-14. Ensuring against power-line flicker.*

All that said, I would enable this function anyway. Use auto if available (it wasn't an option in this software), and select 60 Hz in the US and Japan, and 50 Hz in most other countries.

## Backlight Compensation

If you're running in auto mode and have a bright light behind you, the webcam will reduce the luminance so the light doesn't completely dominate the frame. In most instances, this makes the face too dark, as you can see on the left in Figure 6-15, where backlight compensation is not enabled. When you enable backlight compensation, as shown on the right, the webcam ignores the brightest regions when setting exposure, which brightens the face and the rest of the frame, but also boosts the backlight to very high luminance values.

Backlight compensation is a useful function for a problem that should seldom happen; as you learned in Chapter 3, you should avoid bright lights in the background. When backlights are unavoidable, you should take the webcam off auto mode and adjust the brightness of the image as discussed in previous sections of this chapter.

*Figure 6-15. Backlight compensation (on the right) saves the video.*

That is, backlight compensation isn't doing anything magical; it's simply adjusting exposure/gain or brightness/contrast to boost the luminance of the overall video. By this point, you should be able to produce as good a result or better using manual controls.

## Saving Your Configuration

Once you've achieved visual perfection with your webcam image, you should save the configuration, lest you have to start from scratch and read this entire chapter again (the horror!). Fortunately, most programs make this simple, including the Webcam Settings panel shown in Figure 6-16.

*Figure 6-16. Saving the configuration.*

Click the Save New Profile button on the lower left, and the dialog atop the figure opens. Type in a descriptive name, click Save, and you can turn the page, safe in the knowledge that you'll never have to return to this chapter.

Unless you're working in a studio, lighting and positioning will change slightly with each event, so you should use the preset as a starting point and fine-tune each time. Anytime you change location and/or lighting dramatically, you should start from scratch and create new settings.

## Key Takeaways

- Use auto mode whenever possible, which should be in most cases if you're following the rules for background, clothing and lighting described in previous chapters.

- You may need to manually configure your webcam if the video is too dark or too light; if the color or focus is off; or if the webcam continually adjusts luminance, color, or focus in response to minor changes.

- When adjusting your webcam manually, you'll have to disable auto controls for luminance, color, and (if necessary) focus.

- When adjusting your webcam manually, adjust luminance first, then color, then focus.

- When adjusting luminance, use exposure and gain controls first, if available. If exposure is available but no gain, fine tune your settings with brightness, contrast, and gamma.

- When exposure/gain controls aren't available, brightness and contrast adjustments almost always are, so you'll have to use those controls to adjust luminance. If a gamma adjustment is also available, try that before brightness and contrast.

- When correcting color, adjust hue first until the colors are accurately represented, then adjust saturation.

- When manually setting focus, disable auto-focus, sit in the position you'll use during the conference, and adjust the focus slider until the video is as sharp as possible. Remember that if your position shifts during the conference, you may be out of focus.

# Chapter 7: Choosing a Mic

*Figure 7-1. You don't have to spend a fortune to improve audio quality. Both of these mics are well under $20.*

While we care more about how we look during videoconferences and webinars than how we sound, most of the really valuable information is actually passed via by audio, not video. This makes audio more important than video for virtually all business-oriented productions.

In most instances, you'll produce better audio with an external mic than using the internal mic on your computer, phone, or webcam. You'll learn why and how to choose and use external mics gear in this chapter.

# Overview

In this chapter, you'll learn how to buy external microphones (mics) for your webcam- and smartphone-based productions. I'll start by covering some mic basics, and then branch off into separate discussions about mics to buy for desktop and mobile. First, I'll detail a simple approach for readers looking for a quick boost in quality, essentially covering mics that connect directly into your computer or mobile device and cost less than $100. The final section will cover more complex and expensive solutions for those seeking the absolute top-quality audio.

Major topics include:

- Mic overview

- Choosing a mic: what you need to know

- Plugs and connectors

- Quick and inexpensive options

- Going for absolute top quality.

# Getting Started

When buying a mic, first you should identify the mic type, and then figure out how you're going to connect and power it. If your budget is small, you'll connect it using existing plugs on your computer, which I cover in the Quick and Inexpensive Options section. If your budget is more flexible and you're seeking ultimate quality, you may need a preamp or other adapter to connect and power your mic. I cover that in the final section. But it all starts with the mic type.

There are many, many types of mics, but you're probably familiar with most of them. When choosing a mic, consider two high-level principles.

## Closer is Better

The easiest audio solution for conferencing or webinars is to use the internal mic on your computer, webcam, or mobile phone. Unfortunately, for a number of reasons—including the two to three feet distance between your mouth and the mic—this is almost always the lowest-quality solution.

| Lavalier | Headset | EarPods | Bluetooth |

*Figure 7-2. Closer to the mouth is better.*

Figure 7-2 shows several different mics that get much closer to your mouth than your smartphone, webcam, or computer, which always means better quality. Within the group, each mic has its strengths and weaknesses.

Lavalier mics are the least obtrusive, which makes them the best choice when you're on camera. If echo becomes a problem, you'll have to add earbuds or a Bluetooth mic (see text box, "Echo Cancellation (or Not)").

Moving along, I like headsets for audio-only webinars or conferences when I'm not on camera. Headsets are also handy if echo cancellation either stops working or doesn't exist.

Headsets position the mic close to the mouth and move with the head, so unlike lavalier mics clipped to the collar, they never get out of range. Since the mic is always pointed at the speaker's mouth, a cardioid pickup pattern (explained below) can minimize ambient noise, which is why many sports announcers use these mics.

On the downside, these headsets don't necessary look great on camera. Since they are so close to the mouth, they can produce plosives (popping noises upon Bs and Ps) and sibilants (hissing Ss) and proximity effect, which increases the bass in the spoken word. You can hear some of the plosives in the headset tests available at bit.ly/A1mic.

> ## Echo Cancellation (or Not)
>
> Whenever you engage in a two-way (or multi-way) conference, echo or feedback is possible. That's because speech from other parties coming through your speakers can feed back into your mic, producing echoing or screeching feedback.
>
> Skype and FaceTime use echo-cancellation technologies to avoid this problem, which generally works well, but not 100 percent of the time. In contrast, some conferencing solutions either don't use echo cancellation or haven't worked out all the bugs. That's why I use a headset every time I conference with Google Hangouts.
>
> The bottom line is that echo is a potential problem in any two- or multi-way conference, so you need to be ready. If you don't use a headset or headphones from the start, you should keep one close at hand should echo start to occur.

## Bigger is Better

Another truism is that bigger mics generally produce higher quality than smaller mics—particularly those embedded in phones or computers. Bigger mics have larger diaphragm for sensing the audio and draw more power, enabling higher-quality components.

Although all TV anchors on news and similar shows use lavalier mics, most talk radio personalities use high-end studio mics, like that shown on the far right in Figure 7-3, because they deliver higher-quality sound than lavaliers. Sure, they're big, ugly and obtrusive, and you constantly have to be concerned about speaking into them, but sound is the thing. Along the same vein, many producers of audio-only podcasts also use studio mics.

Beyond these traditional mics, the popularity of mobile video production and conferencing has created multiple new categories of mics. On the left in Figure 7-3 is the IK Multimedia iRig Mic Field, which plugs into the Lightning connector of an iPad or iPhone. Even though it's just as far from the mouth as the device's embedded mic, because it's larger, it delivers a higher-quality signal.

*Figure 7-3. Larger is also better.*

The next two mics to the right are the IK Multimedia iRig Mic HD and Azden SGM-990 shotgun. The handheld mic is larger than the embedded mic in a smartphone, computer, or webcam, and can be positioned closer to the mouth—two significant advantages. It's also very easy to share, which is great when you've got more than one person on the call. The pickup pattern of the shotgun (more on this later) allows it to eliminate ambient noise much more effectively than an embedded mic, producing a higher-quality signal if you're positioned a few feet from the mic.

⚠️ **Caution:** *As of May 2015, none of the conferencing apps I tested worked with mics that connected via the iPhone's Lightning connector. I've included them for completeness, but don't buy one for conferencing unless you absolutely know the program you intend to use supports it.*

To help you assess the qualitative difference between the various options, I've created two web pages with audio recorded using various devices. You can listen to computer-based recordings at bit.ly/A1mic, and mobile recordings at bit.ly/i_mics.

Which mic is right for you? Different horses for different courses, and a lot depends on factors like convenience and portability as well as quality. For what it's worth:

- When videoconferencing from my computer with a webcam, I prefer a lavalier mic with earbuds if needed for echo avoidance.

- For audio-only webinars or conferencing, I prefer the convenience of a headset.

- When I'm conferencing from my phone, I prefer the Apple EarPods for convenience and very good quality.

Going beyond my preferences, some webinar producers prefer large studio mics for the sheer audio quality they can produce. For example, Figure 7-4 shows the audio setup used by Travis White, a colleague who works at NewBlue. I was watching a webinar he produced (bit.ly/mic_setup) and was so impressed with the audio quality that I asked him about his setup. Briefly, he's using a Samson C01 condenser studio mic powered by a vintage Shure M267 mixer/preamp, connected to his Mac with a RadioShack XLR-to-USB adapter.

*Figure 7-4. Audio setup for NewBlue webinars.*

You can see the pop screen in Figure 7-4, which is the mesh filter attached to the top of the mic. Pop screens minimize plosives (popping noises upon

Bs and Ps) which are always a danger for inexperienced mic users. If you're going to use a studio mic, you definitely need a pop screen.

To be clear, the webinar Travis was producing was an audio-only webinar accompanying a software demonstration, so he wasn't on camera, which might have convinced him to use a different mic. That said, most of the talk show hosts I've seen on ESPN and other stations prefer studio mics even when on camera. If you want to produce the absolute best audio quality, a setup like that shown in Figure 7-4 is worth considering.

# Other Buying Considerations

Once you've decided on a form factor, you should next consider the mic's pickup pattern, power, and connection requirements.

## Pickup Pattern

The pickup pattern describes where the mic acquires the bulk of the sound. Figure 7-5 shows the two most common patterns found in mics we'll be discussing: omnidirectional and cardioid.

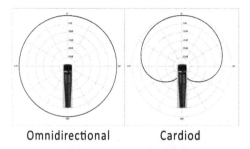

Omnidirectional          Cardiod

*Figure 7-5. The two most common pickup patterns.*
*(Photo courtesy Galak76, Wikimedia Commons.)*

Briefly, omnidirectional mics acquire sound equally from all directions—front and back and all around—while cardioid mics pick up sound primarily from the front of the mic. Some mics have even more focused patterns and are called hypercardioid, which usually means a shotgun mic, like the Azden mic shown in Figure 7-3 (second from the right).

Cardioid is generally preferred for conferencing applications, since speech is very focused and from a single location. With handheld mics, headsets and head-worn mics, cardioid mics are common because they're very easy to position. Obviously, positioning is critical because if the mic is pointed in the wrong direction, the audio signal is diminished.

In contrast, most lavalier mics are omnidirectional because it can be hard to point a lavalier directly at the mouth. In addition, with a cardioid lavalier mic, signal strength will drop when the speaker turns his or her head. There's a wonderful discussion of the strengths and weaknesses of omni versus cardioid mics at bit.ly/omni_or_cardiod. I prefer omnidirectional lavalier mics, but if I were conferencing in a noisy environment, I would try a cardioid unit.

## Power Requirements—Dynamic versus Condenser

Next up are the two basic mic types: dynamic and condenser. Dynamic mics capture audio from the physical vibration of the sound and don't need external power. Condenser mics use electronic components to detect audio and need electric power.

I recommend condenser mics because they usually produce a stronger signal than dynamic. Largely for this reason, most of the mics you've seen above are condenser, which means you have to power them.

Fortunately, you have many options for powering your mics. Most inexpensive mics can draw power from the mic input ports on your computer or smartphone, which you will learn more about below. Some run on tiny batteries, while USB mics draw power from the USB port. For high-end mics, however, you'll probably need a preamp, as you'll learn about in the final section of this chapter.

*tip* *Many smaller mics use a technology called "electret" capsules to capture the sound. Electret mics are all condenser mics that need power to operate. Electret mics with 1/8" (3.5 mm) connectors are often powered via power supplied by mic ports on computers, which is called plug-in power. More on this in a "Short Primer on Plugs," below.*

So, most mics used in videoconferencing are condenser mics that need power—and, of course, you need to plug them in somewhere to access the audio. You'd think this would be simple stuff, but it can get a little confusing, particularly when working with mobile devices and Macs. It's not rocket science, though, so if you can hang through the next couple of sections, it will all fall into place.

## A Primer on Connectors

Figure 7-6 shows the two most common mic connectors. The plug on the left is from the EarPods that came with my iPhone. The three white stripes separate the connector into four channels, called tip, ring, ring, and sleeve, or shortened to TRRS. I know this acronym sounds hyper-technical, but it's really just a way of identifying a connector with four discrete signals.

Specifically, the TRRS connector carries stereo audio out plus a mono mic channel into the iPhone, plus ground as the fourth channel. The important takeaway here is that when you see three lines, it means four channels, and almost always stereo audio out and mono audio in.

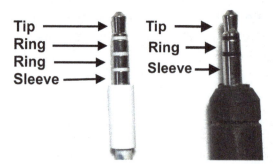

*Figure 7-6. The most common 1/8" (3.5 mm) connectors. This is the standard size connector on most computer headphones and mics.*

The connector on the right in Figure 7-6 has two lines for three channels, and is called a TRS connector because there is a tip, ring, and sleeve. As shown in Figure 7-10, the channels carry left and right audio inputs as well as a ground.

### Stereo Mics Don't Work in TRRS Plugs

As you probably know, you can plug a set of stereo headphones into your iPhone (or Android phone) and you can hear just fine, even though the plug supports four channels and the stereo headphones have three. However, the same isn't true with your stereo mic cable, or even mono mic cable. If you plug either of these into your iPhone, they simply won't work. To use mic with a TRS connector in the iPhone, or an Android phone with four channels, you'll need an adapter, which we'll discuss in Chapter 9.

Just to confuse things even further, there are two different standards for TRRS connectors that carry mic input and stereo output, like that shown on the left in Figure 7-6. These are the Open Mobile Terminal Platform (OMTP) specification, followed by older Android devices and other smartphones, and the Cellular Telephone Industry Association (CTIA) specification, which is used by Apple and most newer (post-2012) Android devices. So not all of these cables are interchangeable. You can read more on this at bit.ly/CTIA_1 and bit.ly/CTIA_2. The bottom line is that if you're buying a headset with a mic and headphones, make sure it's compatible with your device before you buy.

# A Short Primer on Plugs

I started with connectors because you can see the channels that they support, whereas all plugs look alike. There are a couple of important distinctions, however, which you'll learn in this section. Let's start with the audio inputs in most Windows desktops, which are shown in Figure 7-7.

# Mic and Line Input—Windows Computers

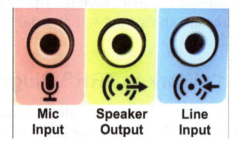

*Figure 7-7. The connections on a typical sound card or desktop computer.*

Figure 7-7 shows the audio plugs on an HP workstation in my office. As you can see, there are three plugs (or jacks): one for mic input, one for speaker output, and one for line input. Here's the difference.

• Mic input (pink). This supplies the electricity to power electret mics like those in inexpensive lavalier, desktop and headset mics (plug-in power). They also expect a very low-volume signal that will be amplified by the sound-related circuits on the motherboard.

• Speaker output (green). This is the connector for the headphones or speakers.

• Line input (blue). This plug is for input from a powered device, like a preamp, audio mixer, or AC-powered mic. This plug won't supply any power and expects high volumes it won't have to amplify.

With notebooks like my HP EliteBook (Figure 7-8), which I frequently use for conferencing, you'll only have one input, which according to the specs (and the tiny icon on the body), is mic input. This does power the electret mics that I use, and with careful adjustment of audio volumes, can also handle input from some pretty "hot" audio sources, like output from a preamp.

> **tip** *In audio-speak, a "hot" audio source means a source with lots of volume, typically from an AC-powered device like a preamp, which is a device that amplifies the incoming signal before it gets to the computer or mobile device.*

*Figure 7-8. Audio plugs on my HP notebook:*
*headphones on the left, mic input on the right.*

The bottom line is, before you plug a mic connector into an input jack, you need to know which type of jack it is, mic or line power. That's simple enough with most Windows computers, but what about Macs?

## Mic and Line Inputs—Macs

Figure 7-9 shows the connectors on my daughter's MacBook Pro. On the left is a line input port, and on the right is a headphone port. Seems simple enough, right? Well, actually no.

*Figure 7-9. Most Macs have a line input and headphone jack.*

That's because the headphone port on the right is essentially the same as the headphone port on an iPhone, and supports four channels: left and right audio out, mic input in, and ground.

So if you plug the EarPods from an iPhone into the headphone jack of most MacBooks, MacBook Pros and Mac Pros, both the headphones and the mic input will work. Like most mic input ports, the Mac's headphone ports supply plug-in power to electret mics, like the tiny one embedded in the Apple EarPod headset.

As discussed previously, you can't plug a typical TRS (dual-mono) mic plug into the headphone jack of a Mac; the physical connection won't work. Rather, you need a TRS-to-TRRS adapters like that shown in Figure 7-12, which I describe below.

## Mobile Inputs

So that's Windows and Mac computers. What about mobile? Most smartphones and tablets have four-signal plugs that support TRRS connectors with stereo audio out and mono audio in, and these plugs supply plug-in power. If you have the headset that came with your device, you're in good shape. If not, you'll need a TRS-to-TRRS adapter.

## Quick Summary on Plugs and Connectors

• When connecting low-power or unpowered 1/8" (3.5 mm) mics into a computer or notebook, use the mic input. Expect to have to amplify the sound, which you'll learn about in Chapter 9.

• When connecting inputs from an AC-powered source, use the line input, if available.

• If you plug inputs from an AC-powered device into a mic input, start with volumes very low. Output volume is likely to be very loud and you don't want to blow your speakers.

• If you plug an electret mic into a line input, you won't hear anything, because the mic won't get powered. This is why electret mics don't work in some consumer camcorders—since the camcorder doesn't supply the power, the mic doesn't capture any sound.

• Mobile phones and Macs have TRRS headphone ports that can accept mono mic input and supply plug-in power. You can use mics or headsets with the TRRS connector, or standard dual-mono mics with an adapter.

## Mono versus Stereo versus Dual Mono

Although all the mics you've seen have different form factors, they share one common characteristic: they're all monaural (mono) mics. Each has one sensing device that picks up a single signal.

*Figure 7-10. A mic producing dual-mono output*

The key issue is how to record mono but provide your listeners with audio in both ears. Figure 7-10 shows how this works with most inexpensive mics; while there is only one mic, there are two outputs. If you can't see it in the figure, pull out a pair of headphones and study the plug. Each of the black (or white) lines separates a channel. If there are two lines, as there in the figure, there are three signals: left audio, right audio, and ground.

The mic in Figure 7-10 captures one mono signal and outputs that same signal to both channels. It's not really stereo as much as dual-mono, since the output from each ear is identical, but the listener is happy because they get a signal out of both speakers or ear buds.

That's the key point. Ninety-nine percent of the time, your audio gear and software will automatically push the same mono signal to the left and right channels—no muss, no fuss. If for some reason your listeners only hear out of one speaker, you have a problem in your audio workflow. In most instances, the cause is a mic with a mono input channel, or one that has only one black or white line (technically a Tip Sleeve, or TS connector). Swap it out for a TRS mic like that shown in Figure 7-10 and you should be OK.

# The Two Sections: Where to Look?

Now you know the high-level basics. There are two approaches to mic purchasing and use: quick and inexpensive, and max quality. Most readers will likely choose the quick and inexpensive route, which I cover first. In that section, I'll cover mics that you can plug directly into your computer or mobile device without a separate device like a preamp, which amplifies the incoming signal before it gets to the computer or mobile device.

These mics are inexpensive and easy to use, and are definitely an improvement over the internal mic of phones, webcams and notebooks. Most of these mics use the familiar 1/8" (3.5 mm) connector or a USB connection. I divide this quick and expensive approach into two sections: one for computers, one for mobile devices.

In the section after that, "Going for Max Quality," I cover options that use preamps to deliver absolute top quality, while costing more and adding complexity to set up and use. Most of these mics use a three-prong connector called the XLR.

# Quick and Inexpensive—PCs/Notebooks

In this section I talk about mics you can connect to your computer or notebook without a special adapter other than a TRS-to-TRRS cable adapter that lets a dual-mono mic work in the headphone port of a Mac. You'll see a picture of such an adapter in Figure 7-12.

Before getting started, note that there are probably a thousand different options, if not more, for choosing and connecting a mic to your computer. My preference is simple: I like a lavalier mic when I'm on a webcam and an analog headset when I'm not. But in this next section I'll provide a quick overview of the type of mics you should be considering.

🗨️*tip* *Just because a mic (or type of mic) works well for me doesn't mean it will work for you. Expect to try multiple mics in multiple form factors before you find one that's perfect for you.*

## Plug-in Powered Mics

Mics that accept plug-in power are the cheapest and easiest way to up the sound quality of your conferencing or video chat. Figure 7-11 shows two products that I use and like a lot: the Neewer 3.5mm lavalier mic (~$7 at Amazon) and the Logitech Stereo Headset H110 (~$8 at Amazon).

*Figure 7-11. Two inexpensive mics that work well for me.*

I mostly conference from my HP notebook, which has a separate mic input with plug-in power, supplying power to both mics (Figure 7-8). I prefer analog headsets to USB or wireless headsets because my voice sounds less synthetic. There's a touch more background noise than with USB headsets, but the voice sounds more natural. You can hear the outputs of several mics in each class at bit.ly/A1mic.

When conferencing from my Mac Pro, I have to pair either mic with a TRS-to-TRRS adapter like that shown in Figure 7-12—which, of course, I plug into the headphone port, not the line-in port. On the left is the TRRS plug that goes into the headphone port of the Mac or mobile device. On the right are two plugs: one for the headphones, one for the mic.

*Figure 7-12. The Azden i-Coustics HX-Mi TRRS adapter.*

This adapter does transfer plug-in power to the mic, so it works with both mics shown in Figure 7-11, both on my Mac and on my iPhone. It costs $20 on Amazon, although I got mine bundled with the Azden WHD-PRO audio kit. Most TRS-to-TRRS adapters cost around $7 or so, and I'm guessing that they transmit plug-in power to the mic, but I can't vouch for it.

> *If you do buy a TRS-to-TRRS adapter, make sure it has both headphone out and mic input. Some are designed for shooting video, not conferencing, and offer one or more mic inputs, but no speaker outputs, which are necessary for conferences. The inputs and outputs should be listed on the product specs.*

## Battery-powered Plug-in Mics

Figure 7-13 shows the battery-powered Audio-Technica ATR3350 mic. You should consider a battery-powered mic if you're having trouble achieving sufficient volume with mics powered via plug-in power. For example, in my testing (bit.ly/A1mic), the ATR3350 produced a stronger signal than any of the electret lavalier mics powered by the mic jack.

Another class of battery-powered mics are wireless headsets, which connect via Bluetooth or small USB keys. Typically, these function much like the USB headset shown in Figure 7-14, but without the physical cable. The wireless headphones that I tested, like the Logitech Wireless Headset H800, sounded synthetic, as does my Plantronics M50 Bluetooth mic. I can't say that all Bluetooth mics have this issue, but it's something to listen for if you do try a wireless headset.

*Figure 7-13. The handy Audio-Technica ATR3350.*

## USB-powered Mics

USB mics include both handheld mic and headsets like that shown in Figure 7-14, which is the Plantronics Audio 478 headset (~$26). Obviously, USB mics draw their power from the USB port you plug them into.

*Figure 7-14. The Plantronics Audio 478 USB headset.*

All of the USB mics I tested were headsets because I find handheld and studio mics awkward for conferencing applications and webinars. If you're interested in these mics, there's a useful roundup of information by Michael Miller at bit.ly/usb_mics.

Although most USB mics are mono, they send the same mono signal to both left and right recording channels, resulting in a stereo (well, dual-mono) signal. So you shouldn't have any problem getting audio in both channels with a USB mic.

*tip Many USB headsets use noise-cancellation technology to dampen ambient noise, which most analog headsets don't have. For this reason, if you're conferencing in a noisy environment, a USB headset may be a better option than an analog headset.*

# Quick and Inexpensive—Mobile

There's a cottage industry devoted to making mics for smartphones and tablets, so you have lots of options. However, many of these mics are for shooting videos or audio recording, not two-way conferencing. When choosing a mic or adapter for mobile use, make sure you choose an option that doesn't block the headphone jack.

I tested my iPhone 6 with a number of mic options that you can hear at bit.ly/i_mics (try the Safari browser if Chrome or another browser won't easily load the QuickTime plug-in). Here's a quick overview of your mobile options.

*tip See "A Primer on Connectors," above, for the definition of TRRS and other plugs. It will just take a moment, and it will make the following sections a whole lot easier to understand.*

## Internal Mic/Supplied Headset

The embedded mic on your smartphone works great for phone calls because it's so close to the mouth, but from 18 to 24 inches away— FaceTime and Skype distance—it provides a weaker signal with lots of background noise. Many mobile devices incorporate TRRS plugs with stereo headphone output and mono mic input, and a headset with a mic, like the Apple EarPods included with the iPhone 6 (Figure 7-15). These do a great job for conferencing, providing a useful, free option.

*Figure 7-15. The mic on the iPhone EarPods does a credible job.*

## Other TRRS Options

There are other options that plug into the TRRS connector of a smartphone or tablet, like the IK Multimedia iRig Mic Cast shown in Figure 7-16, which costs ~$30 at Amazon and has a headphone port on the right, so you can use this mic with ear buds or regular headphones.

*Figure 7-16. The IK Multimedia iRig Mic Cast.*

Mics like these are convenient, and much larger than the iPhone's mic so should pic up a stronger signal. Of course, because they're connected to the phone they're about 24 inches from your face, which could translate to additional noise. I watched several YouTube videos using this mic, however, and the performance was impressive.

*tip* *There are many lavalier mics with TRRS connectors that you can plug into the headphone port on your mobile device. While these work great for shooting video, they typically don't have a headphone jack output, so you can't use them for conferencing.*

## Other TRS Mics

You should be able to use desktop mics like the lavalier and headset with TRS connectors shown in Figure 7-11 if you have the adapter shown in Figure 7-12. I've tested both on my iPhone 6, and the Azden cable did provide the necessary plug-in power to the two mics. Note, however, that incoming mic volume was pretty low. Depending upon your device, you may not be able to boost this, so don't use this combination in a conference or video chat without testing the input volume beforehand.

If you're having trouble getting sufficient volume from an external mic, you can try a battery-powered mic, like the Audio-Technica ATR3350iS shown in Figure 7-17 (~$22 at Amazon). This comes with an adapter with a headphone jack, which is shown atop the figure.

*Figure 7-17. The Audio-Technica ATR3350iS.*

## Bluetooth Headsets

Another mobile option is a Bluetooth headset, which you may already have for phone calls and should work fine with most conferencing apps. Although the Plantronics M50 shown in Figure 7-18 (~$30 at Amazon) I use produces a slightly synthetic sound, it was crisp and clear, and you probably already know how to link it to your cell phone.

*Figure 7-18. The Plantronics M50 produced a crisp, though synthetic, sound.*

*tip* *This is not something I've encountered personally, but occasionally Bluetooth devices can become spotty in crowded environments like a conference center. Just another reason not to hold a videoconference from a conference center.*

## Other Options—iPhone Lightning Connection

There are several inexpensive iPhone/iPad mics that connect via the Lightning connector or older 30-pin connector. Since the Lightning connector can supply more power than the headphone jack, these devices should be able to use higher-quality microphones. One such unit is the IK Multimedia iRig Mic Field shown in Figure 7-19 (~$90 at Amazon).

*Figure 7-19. A convenient Lightning connector-based mic.*

Again, none of the conferencing apps that I tested recognized this, or any other, Lightning connector-based mics. I mention the iRig Field for completeness, but until apps like Skype, FaceTime, or Google Hangouts recognize these mics, don't buy one for videoconferencing.

### Other Options—Android USB Microphones

Most Android smartphones and tablets connect to the computer and recharge via mini-USB ports. For this reason, it would seem that USB mics should work with an Android device. This is true, but only for a limited number of apps, which doesn't include Google Hangouts or Skype according to my tests. This may change over time, of course, but unless you hear to the contrary, I wouldn't assume that a USB mic worked with your Android device for a videoconferencing-type application.

OK, this concludes the quick and inexpensive options. Let's explore some higher-quality, but more expensive and complicated, options.

*Microphones with three-prong XLR connectors, and the devices they connect to, are generally recognized as delivering top quality, especially over long cable lengths. There are multiple theories about what the letters XLR actually stands for, which you can read about at soundfirst.com/xlr.html.*

# Going for Maximum Quality

If you're producing a webinar, or have a conference call with the Queen (metaphorically or actually), you may want to try for absolute maximum quality. Typically, this will involve higher-end equipment including XLR-based mics in multiple configurations and studio mics. This ups the ante in both cost and complexity. In this section, you'll learn how to connect and power XLR-based mics on both computers and mobile devices.

## Connecting XLR Mics

XLR mics are typically used for professional recording in a broad swath of businesses, including broadcast, music, conferences, and other events. XLR-based mics come in many form factors, including handheld, lavalier, and head-worn, although I've never seen an XLR-based headset mic.

As you can see in Figure 7-20, which shows a Shure SM93 lavalier mic, XLR-based mics use a three-plug connector, which delivers a mono signal from the mic. Typically, if you use an XLR-based mic, you'll have to convert the signal to stereo (dual-mono) at some point in the workflow to deliver audio in both the left and right channels. Many of the preamps (more later) used to power these mics can do this, so it shouldn't be a problem.

*Figure 7-20. An XLR-based Shure SM93 lavalier mic.*

Computers and webcams don't have XLR ports, so typically you'll need an adapter or other device to connect the mic to your computer. However, if the mic isn't battery powered, you'll also have to supply 48 volts of power to the mic, which is called phantom power. Making the physical connection isn't enough; you also need the phantom power.

*Figure 7-21. The Hosa Technology XVM-101M connector.*

As an example, consider the adapter shown in Figure 7-21, which is a Hosa Technology XVM-101M, a male XLR to male 1/8" (3.5 mm) stereo audio connector, which costs about $10. Connect that to a battery-powered XLR mic, and you're got a very affordable way to connect an XLR mic to your computer, and convert mono input to dual-mono output. Connect it to an XLR mic that needs phantom power, and you have no output whatsoever. That's why you need a preamp, or other device that can supply that power.

*tip* *If you buy an XLR mic, you'll probably need a male-to-female XLR cable of some length, so don't forget to buy that with the mic. All mics have male XLR outputs (Figure 7-20), so you'll plug the female end into the mic. All preamp plugs are female (Figure 7-22) so you'll plug the male end into the preamp.*

## Powering Your XLR Mic—Preamps

There are many ways to power to XLR mics. I'll discuss two here for computers, and another later for mobile devices.

One product I frequently use for conferencing and webinars is the PreSonus AudioBox 44VSL (Figure 7-22), a preamplifier (preamp) that supplies phantom power and other audio controls. You can read my review of the product at bit.ly/44VSL. Preamps are devices that power mics and amplify the audio volume before it gets to your computer. Although you can boost volume in your computer, preamps produce much higher quality.

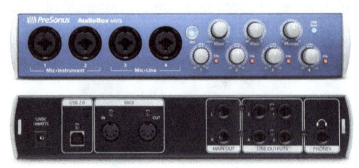

*Figure 7-22. The AudioBox 44VSL preamp.*

With four inputs, the 44VSL costs around $300. If you only need two inputs, you can buy the 22VSL, which costs just under $200. Or you can buy other preamps that cost well under $100.

When buying a preamp for an XLR mic, be sure that it can supply phantom power; most units can, and it should be listed on the spec sheet. I like units with USB output, like the 44VSL, so you input a digital signal into your PC.

If you don't have USB output, you can convert XLR output from the preamp to 1/8" stereo audio for input into your computer's line-in jack with a cable like the Hosa XVM-101M connector shown in Figure 7-21.

## Powering Your XLR Mic—XLR-to-USB Adapters

In addition to preamps, there are several XLR-to-USB adapters that can power XLR mics and feed dual-mono input into the serial port of your computer. Figure 7-23 shows the connection diagram for the Blue Icicle (bluemic.com/icicle). Moving from right to left, you connect the mic to the Icicle via an XLR cable, with a USB cable connecting the Icicle to your computer and supplying phantom power.

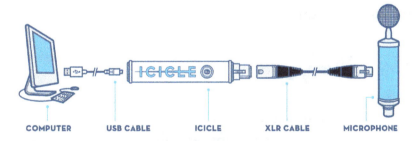

Figure 7-23. Operating schematic for the Blue Icicle XLR-to-USB adapter.

The Shure X2u XLR-to-USB Signal Adapter works similarly to the Blue Icicle (bit.ly/Shure_USB). I have no experience with either product, so check pricing and reviews at Amazon and B&H.

If you're looking for a general-purpose XLR input device, I would consider a preamp like the 44VSL over an XLR-to-USB adapter. If your sole concern is getting audio into your computer for conferencing applications, check out the XLR-to-USB adapters.

### Powering XLR Mics—Mobile Options

What about for mobile applications? There are multiple devices like the IK Multimedia iRig PRE (~$36 at Amazon) shown in Figure 7-24, which can supply phantom power to XLR mics and has the necessary headphone port. This performed well with the Shure SM93 lavalier mic (~$155 at Amazon) I use for most conferences and webinars.

*Figure 7-24. The iRig PRE supplies phantom power to XLR mics.*

Tascam sells a similar product called the Tascam iXZ, which costs around $50 at Amazon. As you'll learn about in subsequent chapters, getting sufficient volume into your mobile device for conferencing is often a concern. A unit like the iRig, which has a separate volume control, can be very useful when mic output is too low.

# Key Takeaways

- Audio carries more data than video in most conferences, so audio quality is critical. An external mic will almost always produce better quality than the internal mic of your computer, webcam, or phone.

- Conferencing applications often experience echo. Keep a pair of earbuds or a headset mic around in case this arises in your calls.

- Most mics are mono; if your listeners hear audio out of only one speaker or headphone, there's a problem in your audio workflow.

- Know your pickup patterns. Cardioid is focused and quieter, whereas omnidirectional picks up sound from all directions.

• Most small mics are condenser mics that need power. Before buying a mic, know how you're going to power it.

• Most computer and mobile mic input jacks provide up to 5 volts of power, sufficient to power inexpensive electret mics found on lavalier mics and some headsets.

• Even if power is provided, if the physical connection doesn't match (plugging a TRS mic into a TRRS connector), the mic won't work.

• Three-connector (XLR) mics need phantom power (48 volts) if they're not independently powered. You'll need a preamp or a device like an XLR-to-USB connector to provide the power.

• Lavalier mics are unobtrusive when you're on camera so are very convenient. Know the pickup pattern, however; omnidirectional mics don't lose volume when you turn your head, but may not function well in a noisy environment. Cardioid mics are better in a noisy environment, but may lose volume when you turn your head or if they're not positioned correctly.

• Headsets are very convenient for audio-only conferences, or when echoing is a problem.

• Studio mics deliver the absolute best quality, but need a pop screen to avoid plosives.

• When conferencing from your phone, the headset that came with your phone is better than the internal mic, as is a Bluetooth headset.

• For absolute top quality with your phone, you can buy an XLR adapter that connects to the headphone port.

• For iOS devices, there are multiple mic options for the Lightning connector, although none of them work for conferencing right now.

• For Android devices, most conferencing programs don't seem to recognize USB mics, so you may be limited to the internal mic and mics that connect via the headphone port.

# Chapter 8: Using Microphones

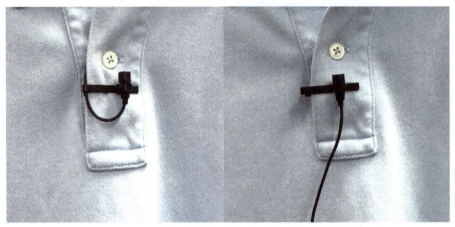

*Figure 8-1. Do this (left), don't do that (right) when wearing a lavalier mic.*

So you just bought the perfect mic for your conferencing task, that's great. But unless you went to broadcasting school, you probably don't know how to use it. Fortunately, it's not that hard.

In this chapter, you'll learn how to use four types of mics: lavaliers, handheld, studio and headset/ headworn. I assume you understand details like the difference between an omnidirectional and cardioid mic, which is covered in Chapter 7. If you don't, start there.

# Overview

Not much drama about what's covered in this chapter; the intro lays it all out. Just to stay consistent with other chapters (and keep the editor off my back), here's the breakdown:

- How to attach and use a lavalier mic
- How to use a handheld mic
- How to use a studio mic
- How to use a headset mic.

If you don't have much experience with mics, you'll find this information both illuminating and useful. Otherwise, I hope it provides a good review.

# Attaching and Using a Lavalier Mic

Lavalier placement is critical to sound quality. Here are the basics.

**Step 1.** Drop the connection end of the mic cable beneath the shirt, leaving 4 or 5 inches of slack at the mic end (or ask the subject you're miking to do so). If there's an XLR connector or wireless body pack, hang it off the subject's belt or put it in a pocket to eliminate pull on the mic cable.

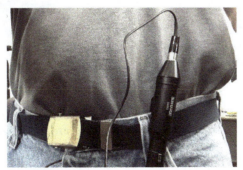

*Figure 8-2. Parking the mini-to-XLR connector on a belt.*

**Step 2.** Place the mic beneath the second button on the shirt. If it's too high, the chin can block the audio and the mic can pickup throat noises. If the mic is cardioid, it must be pointing towards the mouth; if it's omnidirectional, it can point in any direction.

**Step 3.** Create the loop shown on the right in Figure 8-1, which looks tidy and helps prevent noise or worse if the mic is pulled or jerked.

*Figure 8-3. Start here (left). Create a U shape with the wire (right).*

• Shape the wire into a U, bringing the cable into the alligator clip (shown on the right in Figure 8-3).

*Figure 8-4. Loop the cable behind the mic (left) and behind the shirt once it's clipped to the shirt (right).*

• Continue the loop behind the mic and into the alligator clip (shown in the left frame of Figure 8-4).

• Clip the mic on the shirt, making sure to fasten the second loop with the clip on the back of the shirt (Figure 8-4, right).

*Figure 8-5. Adjusting the loop (left). Attaching the mic sideways on a sweater (right).*

• Adjust the cable to eliminate as much as possible from view (Figure 8-5, left). The finished look is on the left in Figure 8-1.

• If you're working with T-shirt or sweater, you can use the same technique except rotated by 90 degrees (Figure 8-5, right).

This looping technique isn't rocket science, but the first couple of times you use it, it takes a few minutes to get right. If you have an event coming up where you'll be miking someone else, practice it a few times on a shirt on a hanger, and you'll be a pro in no time.

⚠️ *Caution! If you're working with a cardioid mic, avoid rotating the mic as shown on the right in Figure 8-5, since this may reduce signal strength. You'll have to find a way to attach the mic pointing upwards, because otherwise you won't produce the necessary volume level and the voice may sound faint.*

⚠️ ***Caution!*** *I know you know this, but if you're attaching the mic on someone else, get permission before you start adjusting, and pull the shirt away from his or her body to minimize physical contact.*

Here are some other lavalier-related considerations.

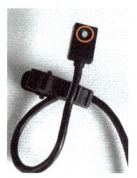

*Figure 8-6. Make sure the mic opening (circled in red) is facing outwards.*

• Make sure the mic opening (the tiny dot in the mic in Figure 8-6) is pointing outwards or upwards, not inwards. If it's inwards, it might rub on the subject's clothing and produce noise. Remove the windscreen (the small fuzzy thing that fits over the mic) if necessary to check where the mic opening is pointing.

• Make sure the mic isn't rubbing against any fabric or other material, which can create contact noise.

• A windscreen might not be necessary in an office environment, but test with and without to determine.

💬*tip* *There's a fabulous free video tutorial on attaching lavalier mics by Anthony Q. Artis at* [bit.ly/attach_lav](bit.ly/attach_lav). *Artis writes the* Shut Up and Shoot *series of books and is a gifted writer, producer and presenter.*

# Using a Handheld Mic

I prefer lavalier mics when I'm on camera, but for an audio-only conference, a high-quality handheld mic can deliver excellent sound. A handheld mic is also a good option when you have to share a mic among two or more people.

*Figure 8-7. Point handheld mics at the speaker's mouth.*

Here are some considerations for using handheld mics.

• Most handheld mics are "top-address" mics, which means you should point the mic directly at the speaker's mouth (as shown in Figure 8-7) at a distance of 6 to 12 inches.

• If the mic is cardioid, pointing the mic towards the mouth is even more important.

• When using a handheld mic for a single user, use a stand that lets the speaker talk comfortably into the mic without bending forward, which is tough to do for longer than 10 minutes.

• Pop screens (or shields) like that shown in Figure 8-7 are the best way to limit plosives (pops at Ps and Bs). There's an informative article on pop shields and why you need them at bit.ly/popshields.

# Using a Studio Mic

Many producers of audio-only presentations and webinars use studio mics for the fabulous quality that they deliver. Here are some considerations for using studio mics.

*Figure 8-8. Studio mics are side-address; be sure you're speaking to the correct side.*

• Most studio mics are "side-address" mics, meaning that you talk into the side of the mic (Figure 8-8).

• The optimal distance from the studio mic is about 6 to 12 inches.

• Cardioid studio mics have a front and a back (Figure 8-9). Typically the front has the logo, while the back has any controls. Obviously, you want to speak into the front.

*Figure 8-9. Studio mics have a front (left) and back (right).*

• Use a stand that lets you talk comfortably into the mic without bending forward, which is tough to do for longer than 10 minutes.

• Pop screens (or shields) like that shown in Figure 8-8 are the best way to limit plosives (pops at Ps and Bs). There's an informative article on pop shields and why you need them at <u>bit.ly/popshields</u>.

## Using a Headset Mic

You should place a headset mic to the side and about 1 to 2 inches from the corner of the mouth. Mics placed in front of the mouth pick up wind noise and plosives (pops at Ps and Bs).

*Figure 8-10. Wear headset or headworn mics off to the side.*

Note that the mic capsule, or opening to the capsule, can sometimes twist off target, particularly on inexpensive headsets. You definitely want the mic pointed at the side of the mouth, so make sure that's so when adjusting the mic. If a windscreen (the fuzzy thing over the mic) is obscuring the mic, you can remove it, adjust mic positioning and then replace it.

*Figure 8-11. The mic opening on this headset is marked with a red dot.*

So now you own your mic and know how to use it. Next chapter, you'll learn how to make sure it's producing the optimal volume.

## Mistakes I Have Made (and How to Avoid Them)

The awful thing about recorded webinars is that you get to hear your mistakes again (and again) once you're done. If you've produced or participated in many webinars, you've made your fair share of mistakes. Here are some of mine so you can avoid making them.

**1.** Never use new audio gear for the first time during a live event. I think it's impossible—or at best, highly unlikely—to get audio right the first time you use a new mic or preamp. So if you've got new gear, check it out thoroughly before you use it in an actual event.

**2.** Run a practice event the first time you're using a new platform. Same deal. It's very hard to get this right the first time and you only have one chance to get a live event right.

**3.** Be careful when you watch your event on another computer while you're recording. It's a great security blanket so you can see what your audience is seeing, but computers make noise and can be distracting, and when you go live the audio will start as well. Either turn the audio off or use earbuds for the second computer.

**4.** Police your environment. There's a checklist on this in Chapter 22, but you can't produce high-quality audio in a noisy environment. Mics can be irritatingly capable of capturing even the most minute background noise, so shut off your heating or AC, all printers, computers, and other gear that makes even an imperceptible hum. Turn off cell phones and landlines, put a Do Not Disturb sign on the door, and if you produce at home, make sure it's not Thursday afternoon in the summer, when the lawn guys come.

# Key Takeaways

This whole chapter is a series of key takeaways, so check each major section for the mic that applies to you. (There; now my editor's happy.)

# Chapter 9: Audio Fundamentals

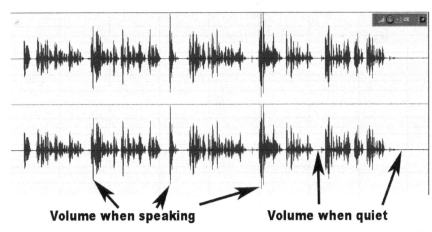

*Figure 9-1. The waveform, a graphical representation of an audio file.*

To produce high-quality audio, you need to know what a waveform is, which is why there's one staring you in the face right now. Briefly, a waveform is a graphical representation of an audio file. Higher peaks in the waveform represent louder audio, lower peaks are quieter, and no peak is no sound at all.

When conferencing, you want your waveform to look like Figure 9-1—loud peaks when you're speaking so your audience can hear you and no sound at all when you're not. In this chapter, you'll learn to produce that kind of audio.

# Overview

This chapter covers fundamentals you need to know when connecting your mics and adjusting volume. Chapters that follow detail these procedures on Windows and Mac computers, as well as iOS and Android devices, and will refer back to lessons learned in this chapter. Specifically, you will learn:

- How to adjust volume, including identifying the target range and adjusting volume, and how to know when you have a problem

- How to connect to a preamp

- How to set volume in an audio chain, or where to adjust volume when you have volume controls on your mic, preamp, operating system, and conferencing software (I know this one has been keeping you up at night, and I'm glad to clear it up for you.)

- What to do if you're scheduled to call into a webinar over the phone.

If your setup is simple, you can stop after the section on volume. If you're using a preamp, you'll probably want to at least skim the final two sections on connecting a mic to a preamp and adjusting volume in the audio chain. Let's get started.

## Volume, Gain, and Levels (Oh My!)

When working with audio, most non-audio professionals—including yours truly—use the terms "volume," "gain," and "levels" interchangeably. At a non-technical level, all three refer to adjusting the perceived loudness of the audio, so the process of adjusting the loudness of your audio could be called adjusting volume, adjusting gain, or setting levels.

To audio professionals, there is a distinction, and there's a useful article on the subject at bit.ly/vol_gain_levels. For our work in this book, I'll use the terms interchangeably, but I will try to use volume most of all for consistency and simplicity.

# Adjusting Volume

We've been adjusting volume all of our live on TV sets, MP3 players, smartphones and tablets, and the radios in our cars. When conferencing, however, rather than adjusting volume to your own liking, you're producing audio to be heard by others—sometimes many others.

To produce the appropriate volume, it helps to understand the tools and interfaces used to produce and analyze audio, and to get a firm view of the appropriate target. So let's start with a discussion of what the desired audio volume is and how to get there.

## What's the Target Volume?

Figure 9-2 shows three waveforms, one of which you saw in Figure 9-1. The volume (or levels) on the top waveform are too low. Listeners will have to boost the volume on their computers or phones to hear you—and even then they may not be able to understand you.

The middle waveform, which you saw in Figure 9-1, is just right. The peaks of the signal touch the top and bottom of the scale, which makes for easy listening, while the midline is free from noise, which boosts comprehension.

The bottom waveform shows the peaks of the signal scrunched up against the top of the scale. This is called peaking or clipping, and it can cause noticeable distortion. The midline is also slightly bushy, meaning background noise has crept into the audio—either because you've boosted gain too much or because you're producing in a noisy environment. Your listeners can hear you, but they may have trouble understanding what you're saying. Not good.

Hopefully, these three waveforms help you visualize the target. You want audio levels that touch or get very near to the tippy top of the scale, but only for a millisecond or two. You want absolute quiet when no one is speaking, and volume somewhere near or above the midline most of the time.

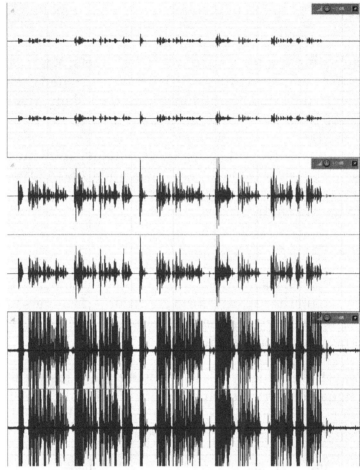

*Figure 9-2. A tale of three waveforms. The one in the middle is just right.*

To accomplish this, you'll adjust volume sliders in various locations, like on the mic or preamp, or in the conferencing software or operating system. I'll describe how to do that in a moment. With many of the better tools, you'll use a volume meter like that shown in Figure 9-3 to help set levels. So let's look at our target on the volume meter.

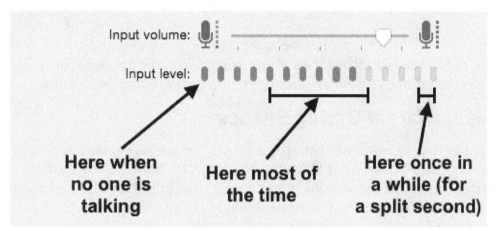

*Figure 9-3. Targets on a volume meter from OS X Sound Preferences.*

When adjusting volume (or setting levels), there are two conditions you want to monitor: normal speech and silence.

## Volume Target During Normal Speech

You'll set the volume in different places for Windows and Mac computers, and iOS and Android devices. I'll specify where and will present specific procedures for setting volume in each of the following four chapters.

At a high level, you open a software program or application, and then you start talking and adjust volume controls to achieve the desired targets. As an example, on the Mac, you would use the controls shown in Figure 9-3, which is in the Sound Preferences.

When you're talking normally, the levels should bounce around in the mid-to-upper zone shown in Figure 9-3. You should also just barely touch the top of the scale (kissing the peaks) every once in awhile, but the meter should never park there.

This produces adequate volume that should be easily discernible by your listeners. As we saw on our waveforms, if the levels are too low, the audio is hard to hear, and if they're too high, the audio gets distorted.

*tip* *When setting levels, duplicate the setup you'll use for your conference or webinar as much as possible. For example, attach a lavalier mic to your chest, or position a studio mic on its stand.*

## Volume Target During Silence

Once the talking levels are set, stop talking. The volume should flicker at a very low level; none at all would be preferred, because any sound is obviously noise. If the volume meter shows substantial levels when no one is talking, you'd produce a waveform that looks like Figure 9-4. Peak levels here are OK, but the bushiness around the midline is pure noise.

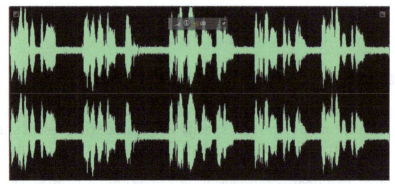

*Figure 9-4. The peaks are OK in this waveform, but there's too much noise around the midline.*

When this happens, you have one of three problems:

• A noisy room. If you have the air conditioning on, white noise in the room, or traffic outside, your mic is picking this up. To produce the best audio, conduct your conference in a quiet environment.

• Too much volume. Back off the volume somewhere in the audio chain, whether the mic, preamp, or operating system software. The risk here is that you may lose the level in your peaks.

• Bad audio equipment or a problem with your gear, particularly if the noise is a whine or obvious static.

An all-too-common problem with cheap audio gear is that you can't achieve sufficient volume while the speaker is talking without too much residual noise when they're not. If you're ever heard a sound person talk about the inability to achieve "sufficient levels" with a mic, this is exactly what they're talking about. I've experienced this more times than I care to remember, and it's why ultimately I moved to a preamp-based system.

So if you find yourself unable to produce sufficient levels without also introducing excessive noise, don't assume you're doing anything wrong. You might just need better equipment.

As a quick summary, here's a procedure to follow when setting levels:

• Start talking and adjust volume to make sure levels stay above 50 percent most of the time and hit the upper regions of the volume meter occasionally.

• Once you reach the target level, stop talking and note how much noise the system is picking up.

• The best procedure is to actually record an audio file while setting levels to gauge the volume and perhaps even see the waveform. I'll discuss programs to use in each of the four chapters that follow.

⚠️*Caution! If you're adjusting volume during the event, you want to set levels once and leave them in that position until something changes, like a different speaker coming on. You don't want to constantly "ride the levels" because this is distracting to listeners. Find a good level that achieves the targets discussed above and leave it alone.*

# Working with Preamps and Audio Chains

If you're using an inexpensive electret mic with no volume controls, your work in this chapter is done; adios. You can learn to connect your mic and set volume in your environment of choice in one of the next four chapters.

If you're seeking absolute top audio quality with an XLR mic and preamp, you'll need to stick around to learn how to connect a mic to a preamp, which is the following section. Once you have the mic and preamp selected, you have one or two volume controls on the preamp, in addition to volume controls in the operating system or conferencing software like that shown in Figure 9-3.

Here your situation transitions from having a single volume control to having multiple volume controls on the different hardware and software components that make up your audio chain. The last major section in this chapter details how to adjust volume within the audio chain. Let's start by getting you connected.

## Connecting a Microphone to a Preamp

Here, I assume that your mic requires phantom power. I'll demonstrate with the Shure SM93 lavalier mic and the PreSonus AudioBox 44VSL, a combination I use frequently for conferencing and webinars. I'll assume that you've got the preamp powered up and ready to go, and the necessary XLR cable to connect the mic to the preamp.

***Step 1. Connect the mic to the cable.*** If you're working with a studio or handheld mic, plug the XLR cable directly into the mic. If you're working with a lavalier mic like the SM93, it will come with a cable that ends with a female XLR connector like that shown on the right in Figure 9-5.

**Mic Cable**          **XLR Cable**

*Figure 9-5. Connect the mic to the XLR cable.*

***Step 2. Connect the cable to the preamp.*** Plug the other end of the cable, which will look like the male XLR connector on the left in Figure 9-5, into the preamp. Use the first open slot.

**Step 3. Enable phantom power.** Typically, there's a button or switch like that shown in Figure 9-6.

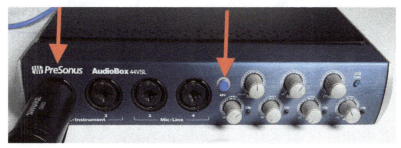

*Figure 9-6. Plug the mic in and enable phantom power (48V blue dot).*

**Step 4. Connect the preamp output to computer.** Depending upon the preamp, there are multiple ways to do this. Here are the most common:

• *USB connection from preamp to computer.* Some preamps, like the 44VSL, offer USB output you can send directly to the computer. This produces the best quality, but is also the most complicated, because you'll have to load drivers for the preamp on the computer. Preamp software is targeted for audio techies, and can be pretty daunting for many users.

• *Main XLR or 1/4" output to line (preferred) or mic input.* Most preamps use either XLR or 1/4" outputs, so you'll need a cable or connector to convert that to a 1/8" (3.5 mm) connector you can plug into the line or mic input on your computer (the 1/8" connector is the standard-sized connector on computer headphones and mics). If the output is XLR, you'll need a connector like the Hosa Technology XVM-101M shown on the left in Figure 9-7. If it's 1/4", you'll need a connector like that shown on the right in Figure 9-7, along with a stereo RCA-to-3.5 mm audio cable.

*Figure 9-7. On the left, an XLR-to-1/8" cable. On the right,
a mono-1/4"-to-stereo-RCA adapter.*

• **XLR output to XLR-to-USB adapter.** We discussed this in a
section entitled "Powering Your XLR Mic—XLR-to-USB Adapters"
in Chapter 7. Briefly, these are devices with an XLR input on one end
and a USB connector on the other.

> *I detail the differences between line and mic inputs back in
> Chapter 7 in a section entitled "A Short Primer on Plugs."*

Which output is best? Technically, the USB output (if the preamp supports
it) is cleanest, since it's a direct digital transfer from preamp to computer.
All the other outputs involve extra digital-to-analog conversions to get the
audio signal out of the preamp, and another analog-to-digital conversion to
get the audio into the computer. As a practical matter, it's unlikely that you
could tell the difference. I use USB output when conferencing from my Mac
Pro, and main output on my HP notebook.

The important thing is to understand which preamp controls affect which
outputs. For example, on the 44VSL, the Main knob controls volume going
out the main outputs, but not the headphone output, which is controlled by
the Phones knob shown in Figure 9-6. Interestingly, neither knob adjusts
the volume of the USB output, so adjusting the gain on the mic input is the
only option on the preamp when connecting via USB.

> ⚠ **Caution!** *Turn down the gain and volume levels on your
> preamp before connecting cables to your computer or mobile device,
> particularly if connecting to a mic input plug. Otherwise, you could
> be in for a very loud surprise when audio starts to pump through.*

## Adjusting Volume in the Audio Chain

By "audio chain," I mean the flow of audio from recording to listening, as shown in Figure 9-8. Every step along the way there is a volume or gain control, or both.

For example, in the figure, there's a mic, a preamp and a Mac with the conferencing application, and all three might have volume controls. The audio gets compressed and sent to over the cloud to the listener, who's on a PC that also has a volume control. The question is, if the volume coming in from the mic is low, where should you boost the volume?

*Figure 9-8. Audio chain. (Adapted from a figure in Wikipedia.)*

It's a question I've often wondered about, but never tracked down. After a bit of research, I found this in a Lectrosonics white paper ([bit.ly/audiochain](bit.ly/audiochain)):

> The amplification of any type of signal is commonly referred to as applying gain. ... In an audio chain, the maximum S/N (signal-to-noise) ratio is achieved when gain is applied at the beginning of the signal chain, and subsequent stages are at unity gain (no increase or decrease).

So, you get the highest quality if you adjust volume once at the beginning of the signal chain—in the case of Figure 9-8, the mic—and that's it. This makes perfect sense because boosting volume always creates some level of noise, and subsequent amplification of noise creates even more noise. To avoid this, you should boost volume to the required levels at the earliest possible stage.

*tip* *The term "unity gain" means the setting that doesn't increase or decrease the volume coming into the device or computer. This concept is important in an audio chain because you're trying to adjust gain as few times as possible within the chain. So you start with all volume and gain controls at unity value, and adjust them to add volume only when necessary.*

*Figure 9-9. Various volume controls on the 44VSL.*
*Where do I boost volume?*

I'll detail procedures for adjusting volume in the audio chain in each of the chapters to follow. In general, the rules are to start at unity value for all volume controls, and then:

- Increase volume on the mic first (if available)

- Then increase the mic input gain on the preamp (if needed)

- Then increase main input volume on the preamp (if needed)

- Then increase gain in the software on the capture station (if needed)

- Then increase volume on receiving end (if needed).

That's it. Now let's move on to the platform-specific chapters, starting with Windows.

## Before Calling into a Webinar

With some audio-only webinar services, you don't send audio from a computer or webcam, you dial in over the phone. This involves multiple layers of compression—once for the phone, another for the web—and audio quality is often noticeably degraded.

If you're scheduled to produce a webinar by phone, ask the webinar provider if there's another option. For example, I recently produced a webinar for Onstream Media using their new Dolby Voice solution. As compared to the previous webinar I had produced for them via phone, the audio was dramatically better.

You can see that in the waveforms below from the recorded versions of the webinars. On the left, the waveform from the phone call shows a lot of bushiness around the midline, which is noise that's painful to listen to. On the right, the Dolby Voice midline is clean, and the upper waveforms crisper and more distinct, indicating noise free audio that's easy to understand.

If you must dial in via phone, never use a cell or VOIP. Always use a landline, with a headset if at all possible, never a speakerphone.

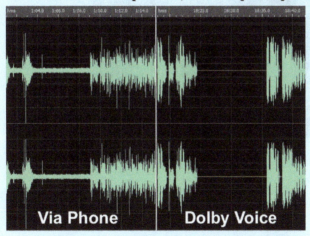

*Figure 9-10. Dolby Voice is cleaner than phone input.*

## A Brief Bit on Signal-to-noise Ratio

Technically, the signal-to-noise (S/N) ratio of an audio device like a preamp is exactly what it sounds like: the ratio of the signal it outputs compared to the noise. Higher ratios are better, so a preamp with a S/N ratio of 97 dB (for decibels) should produce better audio than one with a S/N ratio of 80 dB. That's all well and good, though a bit sterile in application.

I find the vision shown in Figure 9-11 a more helpful use of S/N ratio. When I produce audio, I want the maximum signal when I'm speaking and absolute silence when not. My production goal is always to maximize the signal, and minimize the noise.

Anyone who's ever produced audio will tell you this can be devilishly hard to achieve, but it is possible. So don't be afraid to keep testing new gear in search of this goal, and once you find a setup that works, use it till it breaks.

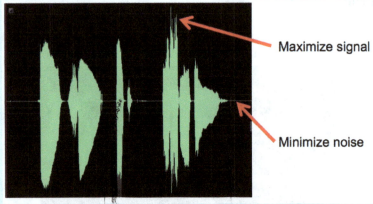

*Figure 9-11. My perpetual audio production goal.*

# Key Takeaways

• Follow this procedure when setting mic levels:

◇ Start talking and adjust volume to make sure levels stay above 50 percent most of the time and hit the upper regions of the volume meter occasionally.

◇ Once you reach the target level, stop talking and note how much noise the system is picking up.

◇ The best procedure is to actually record an audio file while setting levels to gauge the volume and perhaps even see the waveform. I'll discuss programs to use in each of the four chapters that follow.

• Follow these rules when working with an audio chain:

◇ Start at unity value for all volume controls.

◇ Increase volume on the mic first (if the mic has a volume control).

◇ Then increase the mic input gain on the preamp (if needed).

◇ Then increase main input volume on the preamp (if needed).

◇ Then increase gain in the software on your computer or mobile device (if needed).

◇ Then increase volume on receiving end (if needed).

• When producing an audio-only webinar, talking over the phone may not be your best option. Be sure to explore other options with your webinar provider as early as possible.

# Chapter 10: Working with Audio in Windows

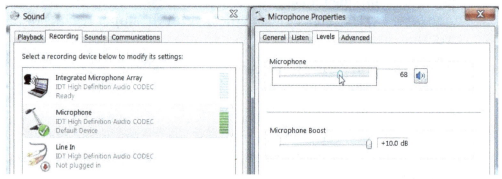

*Figure 10-1. Setting the volume in the Microphone Properties dialog.*

In this chapter, you'll learn how to connect your mic to your Windows computer or notebook, how to select the mic in Windows, and where and how to adjust volume.

# Overview

The major sections in this chapter cover:

- Connecting your mic to a Windows computer or notebook

- Choosing the mic as the default mic within Windows

- Setting volume—simple case (no preamp)

- Setting volume—complex case, with preamp.

Much of the content in this chapter builds on information presented earlier. In particular, if you skipped it, you can learn about line and mic inputs in the section entitled "A Short Primer on Plugs" in Chapter 7.

# Getting Connected

Step 1 is getting your mic connected. Let's start with mics with a 1/8" (3.5 mm) connector, which is the standard-sized connector on computer headphones and mics. This would include the three mics shown in Figure 10-2: the lavalier mic on the left, the headset I'm connecting in the middle, or the battery-powered Audio-Technica ATR3350 mic shown on the right.

*Figure 10-2. Three low-power mics with 1/8" (3.5 mm) connectors.*

The lavalier and headset mics require plug-in power, while the mic on the right is battery powered, which means relatively low power. This means that you should plug all three into the mic input port on your computer or notebook, not the line in.

*Figure 10-3. Typical notebook connectors on the left, typical desktop connectors on the right.*

Figure 10-3 shows the typical connectors on notebooks and desktop computers. Some things to note:

• When connecting an unpowered or low-powered mic like those shown in Figure 10-2, connect to the mic input.

• When connecting the output from a preamp, use line input when available, which it isn't on the left.

• When connecting the output from a preamp and line input is not available, try the mic input, but keep output volumes from the preamp very low to start.

*You can learn about the differences between line and mic power in the section entitled "Mic and Line Input—Windows Computers" in Chapter 7.*

## USB-powered Microphones

Nothing to this; just plug the mic into any USB port and it should work. It may take a moment or two for the Windows driver to setup, but you shouldn't have to do anything to make this happen.

## XLR-to-USB Connectors

There are multiple XLR-to-USB devices that can connect to and supply phantom power to XLR mics, and you can typically use these in Windows computers. I mention two devices in Chapter 7: the Blue Icicle and the

Shure X2u XLR-to-USB adapter. There's a very useful video for the X2u at bit.ly/Shure_X2u that explains the hardware and software setup process. It's worth watching even if you buy a different adapter.

Whichever connection you use, get the mic powered up and plugged in so Windows will recognize it. Now you're ready to choose the mic in Windows.

# Choosing a Mic in Windows

A couple of points before we jump in. First, in most instances, once you attach a new mic to a Windows computer or notebook, Windows will make that mic the default mic. So you may not have to manually select the mic.

Second, some programs, like Skype, let you choose the mic and set volume within their interface. Typically these controls are easier to use and more comprehensive than those provided by Windows, so if they're available, use them. I show you how to access those controls for Skype in Chapter 19.

When you're working with other conferencing applications, check if you can choose and configure a mic within their user interfaces. If so, do it there. If not, as with Google Hangouts, follow these procedures.

**Step 1.** On the bottom right of the task bar, next to the clock, right-click the speaker icon and choose Recording Devices (Figure 10-4).

*Figure 10-4. Right-click the speaker icon on the lower right of your Windows desktop.*

**Step 2.** The Sound dialog opens with the Recording Tab open (Figure 10-5). Right-click the target mic and choose Set as Default Device. Windows will make the selected mic the default.

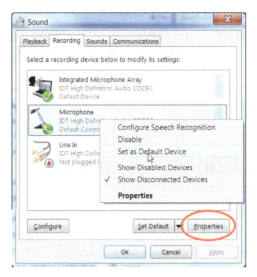

*Figure 10-5. Choosing the default mic.*

Note the volume meters to the right of the inputs in Figure 10-5. We'll use these to set volume in the next section.

*If you have multiple mics installed, they will all appear in the Recording tab shown in Figure 10-5. Just pick the one you want to use as shown.*

## What to Do if You Don't See Your Mic

In my experience, Windows has gotten really good at finding mics and other devices that you've properly installed. If Windows doesn't see your mic, here's a list of things to try:

• Unplug and replug the mic.

• Make sure you're plugged into the right input. Windows might not recognize an electret mic plugged into a line input.

• Check your connector. Windows might not recognize a TRRS connector plugged into a standard mic or line input. More on this in "A Primer on Connectors" in Chapter 7.

*tip* *You should read "Adjusting Volume" and related sections in Chapter 9 before starting this next exercise.*

# Setting Volume—No Preamp

Now that you've selected the mic, let's set the volume. In this instance, I'll assume that you don't have a preamp or other place to boost audio volume except on the mic and within Windows.

**Step 1.** In the Windows Sound dialog, click the mic input to select it, and then click Properties (bottom of Figure 10-5) to open the Microphone Properties dialog. Or, just double-click the mic input and the Microphone Properties dialog opens (on the right in Figure 10-6).

**Step 2.** Click the Levels tab to expose those controls, and drag the Microphone Properties dialog to the right so you can see the volume meters in the Sound dialog (on the left in Figure 10-6). Start with the levels as shown in the figure; note that not all mics will have Microphone Boost.

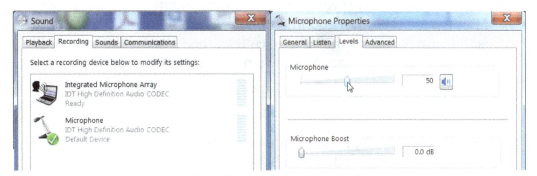

*Figure 10-6. The volume meters in Windows are tiny.*

**Step 3.** Start speaking normally into the mic. If your mic has a volume control, watch the levels in the Sound dialog and increase volume until levels reach the targets. Stop and back off if you start to hear distortion.

*tip* *If you're really concerned about mic volume, try making a test call with Skype. You'll get to hear exactly how you sound to a remote listener. I describe how in Chapter 19.*

**Step 4.** If the mic gain didn't boost volume to the target levels or doesn't have volume controls, drag the volume slider in the Levels tab to the right.

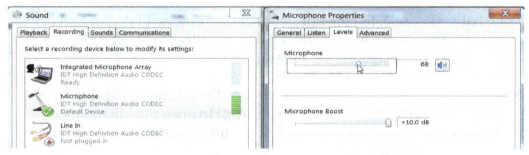

*Figure 10-7. Adjusting volume in the Levels tab. Note volume levels showing on the left next to the Microphone input.*

The controls in the Levels tab vary depending on which port you connect to, as follows:

• **Mic input port.** If you plug into the mic input port, you'll see both Microphone (volume) and Microphone Boost controls. Note that 50 is the unity value for the volume control (no increase, no decrease), which is where you want to be when you start this exercise.

• **Line input port.** If you plug into the line input port, you'll see a single volume control labeled Line In, with no boost control.

• **USB mic.** If you plug a mic into the USB port, you'll see a single volume control labeled Microphone In, with no boost control.

When available, Microphone Boost adds gain to the mic input in chunks of 10 dB (decibels). If boost is available, start with that at the zero value and try to reach the target solely with the Microphone volume adjustment; use boost only when absolutely necessary. If boost isn't available, you're limited to the volume adjustment.

*If you have an audio editor like Adobe Audition or Sony Sound Forge, set levels while recording in the program. You can watch the waveform during recording and listen to it to gauge quality. I would not use Windows Sound Recorder for this because the levels presented are tiny and wildly inaccurate.*

**Step 5.** Stop talking and check the input level, which should show very little volume—one green bar or less in the microphone volume indicator. If it shows more, there's noise in the audio. This can be caused by a noisy environment, too much volume boost, or malfunctioning audio gear.

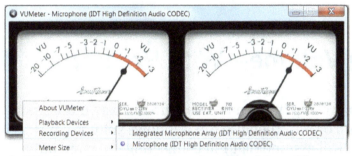

*Figure 10-8. Windows VU Meter is functional and free. The popup window shows how you select the right microphone.*

*If you don't want to record a waveform, consider downloading an application like Windows VUMeter (VU stands for volume units; Figure 10-8), which mimics old-style analog meters and provides better feedback than the Windows Sound dialog. It's free to download at www.vuplayer.com/other.php. When using an analog-style meter, the target should be between -2 and + 2; otherwise your levels will be too low. You can learn more about the difference between digital and analog-style meters at bit.ly/monitor_audio.*

# Setting Volume—With Preamp

If you have a preamp in the mix, you'll first boost volume using controls on the preamp or mic, then use the Windows volume controls if necessary. This exercise will assume that I'm connecting the main output from the PreSonus AudioBox 44VSL preamp to the mic input on my HP notebook, and that the mic doesn't have a gain control. If I were connecting to a desktop computer that had a line input, I would use that input. The exercise would be the same, but I would expect to have to increase the volume on the preamp more when feeding into the line input because it's expecting a louder signal than the mic input.

**Step 1.** On the preamp, set input gain to 0, main output to unity value (Figure 10-9). If the mic had gain control, I would set input gain on the preamp to unity value and start by adjusting mic gain.

**Main - Unity Value**

**Mic Input Gain - 0**     **Clipping Indicator**

*Figure 10-9. The PreSonus AudioBox 44VSL with input gain at 0 and Main at unity value. The four knobs on the bottom control gain for the four inputs. Main output controls volume for the main outputs on the back of the unit, while Phones does the same for the headphones. Mixer controls are particular to this model, so please ignore if you're using a different preamp.*

**Step 2.** In the Windows Sound dialog, click the mic input to select it, and then click Properties (Figure 10-5) to open the Microphone Properties dialog. Or, just double click the mic input and the Microphone Properties dialog opens.

**Step 3.** Drag the Microphone Properties dialog to the side so you can see the volume meters in the Sound dialog (Figure 10-10).

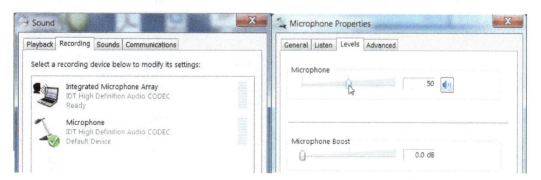

*Figure 10-10. Here we are ready to start adjusting volume.*

**Step 4.** Start speaking normally into the mic.

**Step 5.** Increase mic gain on the preamp until the volume is in the target zone. If the clipping indicator on the preamp (Figure 10-9) starts blinking before you reach the target, reduce gain to eliminate clipping.

**Step 6.** If necessary, adjust the main knob (Figure 10-9) on the preamp to increase volume to achieve the desired target.

**Step 7.** If you still can't achieve the desired levels, you'll have to use Windows' volume control (Figure 10-10) in the Levels tab to achieve the necessary volume. The controls in the Levels tab vary depending upon which port you connect to, as follows:

> • *Mic input port.* If you plug into the mic input port, you'll see both Microphone (volume) and Microphone Boost controls. Note that 50 is the unity value for the volume control (no increase, no decrease), which is where you want to be when you start this exercise.

> • *Line input port.* If you plug into the line input port, you'll see a single volume control labeled Line In, with no boost control.

> • *USB mic.* If you plug a mic into the USB port, you'll see a single volume control labeled Microphone In, with no boost control.

When available, Microphone Boost adds gain to the mic input in chunks of 10 dB (decibels). If boost is available, start with that at the zero value and try to reach the target solely with the Microphone volume adjustment; use boost only when absolutely necessary. If boost isn't available, you're limited to the volume adjustment.

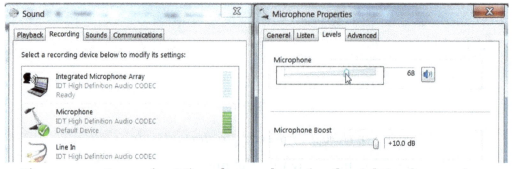

*Figure 10-11. Increasing Microphone volume (on the right) to boost volume to the target values (on the left).*

***Step 8.*** Stop talking and check the input level, which should show very little volume—one green bar or less in the microphone volume indicator. If it shows more, there's noise in the audio. This can be caused by a noisy environment, too much volume boost, or malfunctioning audio gear.

## What the Heck is a Clipping Indicator?

Most preamps have lights that blink if input volumes exceed a threshold that would produce clipping at the peaks of the audio signal, potentially causing distortion. When adjusting volume with a preamp, you can boost the volume until the light blinks frequently, then back off until it blinks very infrequently, if at all.

# Key Takeaways

• Most Windows desktops have separate mic and line inputs; many Windows notebooks only have mic inputs. In most instances, both ports are TRS connectors.

• Connect mics that need power to the mic input; supply connections from preamps and other powered sources into the line input jack.

• Most USB-powered mics should work on Windows computers and notebooks, as should XLR-to-USB adapters.

• Some conferencing apps allow you to choose and configure audio from within their user interface. When available, use these, because they're typically easier to use and more functional than the default Windows controls.

• When you plug in most mics, Windows will automatically make the new mic the default.

# Chapter 11: Working with Audio on the Mac

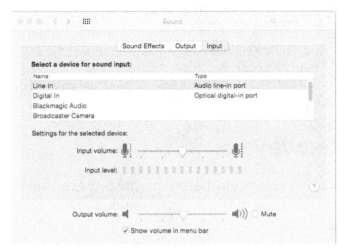

*Figure 11-1. Setting audio volume in Sound Preferences.*

In this chapter, you'll learn how to connect your mic to your Mac computer or notebook, how to select the mic within OS X, and where and how to adjust volume.

# Overview

The major sections in this chapter cover:

- Understanding the ports on a Mac computer or notebook
- Connecting mics to a Mac computer or notebooks
- Choosing the mic as the default mic on the Mac
- Setting volume—simple case (no preamp)
- Setting volume—complex case, with preamp.

Much of the content in this chapter builds on information presented earlier. If you skipped it, I describe what a TRRS plug is in Chapter 7, in a section entitled "A Primer on Connectors." In addition, you can learn about line and mic inputs in the section entitled "A Short Primer on Plugs" in Chapter 7. If you don't know what a TRS-to-TRRS adapter is, go back and read that section.

# Mac Audio Ports

You learned about Mac audio ports back in Chapter 7, but let's review. Figure 11-2 shows the audio ports on a MacBook; there is a line input on the left and TRRS headphone port with mono mic input on the right.

*Figure 11-2. Audio ports on a MacBook Pro.*

This means that the headphone port is functionally identical to the TRRS port found on iPhones, which means that it can play stereo audio, accept mono audio input, and supply power to a mic that requires plug-in power.

There's one caveat: for the mic to work, the plug that connects to the headphone port must be identical to the plug on iPhone EarPods shown on the left in Figure 11-3. Actually, it can be your iPhone EarPods; plugged into the headphone port of your Mac computer or notebook, these can serve as both mic and headset.

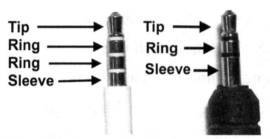

*Figure 11-3. iPhone headset on the left, regular mic jack on the right.*

Architecturally, Apple's strategy is very elegant; you get line in, mic in and headphones out in only two plugs. However, it has several implications on your gear selection and connection, as follows:

• You should plug 1/8" (3.5 mm) connectors from preamps and other AC-powered devices into the line input port.

• If you plug an iPhone-compatible headset with a TRRS connector into the headphone port, the mic and headphones will work.

• Regular TRS mics that require plug-in power, like that shown on the right in Figure 11-3, will not work without an adapter.

• When buying a TRS-to-TRRS adapter, be sure it can supply plug-in power to the mic, and that it has a headphone plug. The Azden i-Coustics HX-Mi TRRS adapter shown in Figure 11-4 meets both these criteria, but costs $20. There are probably adapters in the $7 range that also meet both criteria, but I haven't tested them.

*Figure 11-4. The Azden i-Coustics HX-Mi TRRS adapter.*

*tip* *If you buy a mic adapter for your Mac or iPhone, make sure it has both a mic in port and headphone out ports. Some adapters are designed for shooting video, not conferencing, so don't have a headphone port.*

# Getting Connected

With this as background, let's look at the three mics shown in Figure 11-5. The mic on the left is an inexpensive lavalier that requires plug-in power and won't work if plugged directly into either port on the Mac. It will work with the adapter shown in Figure 11-4, as will the analog headset shown in the middle.

*Figure 11-5. Three low-power mics with 1/8" (3.5 mm) connectors.*

Lastly, on the right, is the Audio-Technica ATR3350, a battery-powered mic that will work with the adapter shown in Figure 11-4. Consider the ATR3350 if you're having trouble producing the necessary volume with other mics powered only by the voltage supplied by the mic input jack.

Note that Audio-Technica sells a version of the ATR3350 with a TRS-to-TRRS adapter with a headphone jack, which is called the ATR3350iS (bit.ly/ATR_iphone).

## USB-powered Microphones

To connect a USB mic to a Mac computer, just plug it into any USB port and it should work. It may take a moment for OS X to recognize the mic, but you shouldn't have to do anything else.

## XLR-to-USB Connectors

There are multiple XLR-to-USB devices that can connect to and supply phantom power to XLR mics, and you can typically use these on Macs. I mention two devices in Chapter 7: the Blue Icicle and the Shure X2u XLR-to-USB adapter.

Whichever connection you use, connect and power up the gear so that your Mac recognizes the mic. Then you're ready to choose that mic in OS X

# Choosing a Mic in OS X

A couple of points before we jump in. First, in some instances, but not all, once you attach a new mic to a Mac computer or notebook, OS X will make the new mic the default mic.

Second, some programs, like Skype, let you choose the mic and set volume within their interface. Typically these controls are easier to use and more comprehensive than those provided in OS X, so if they're available, use them. I show you how to access those controls for FaceTime in Chapter 14, and Skype in Chapter 19.

When you're working with other conferencing applications, check if you can choose and configure a mic within their user interfaces. If so, do it there. If not, as with Google Hangouts, follow these procedures.

With that as prologue, here's how to choose the mic in OS X. For this example, I've connected my Apple EarPods to the headphone jack of a MacBook Pro.

*tip* *If the speaker icon doesn't appear in the menu bar, you can open Sound Preferences from the System Preferences panel.*

**Step 1.** Press the Option key and click the sound icon in the menu bar on the upper right. If the right mic isn't selected, scroll down and choose it.

*Figure 11-6. Mic selection before I plugged in the EarPods (left), and after (right).*

On the left in Figure 11-6, I captured the screen before I plugged in the EarPods, and the internal mic was selected. After I plugged in the EarPods, OS X switched to the external mic. If the desired mic isn't selected, just scroll down and select it.

*tip* *My testing wasn't exhaustive, but OS X didn't seem to make a USB headset I connected the default mic or output device when I plugged them in (Figure 11-7). No worries, just choose the headset as the Input Device and Output Device as described above.*

*Figure 11-7. I had to manually choose the USB headset device I tested.*

**Step 2.** Scroll down and choose Sound Preferences (Figure 11-8).

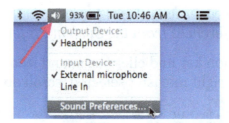

*Figure 11-8. Opening Sound Preferences dialog.*

OS X opens the Sound Preferences on the Input tab (Figure 11-9).

> *If you're installing a headset and want to listen through the headset speakers, click the Output tab atop the Sound dialog, and click the headset to select it.*

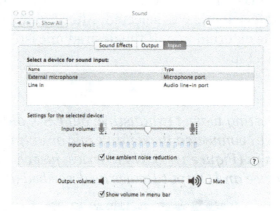

*Figure 11-9. The Sound Preferences dialog, where you adjust volume.*

We'll use this dialog to adjust incoming audio volume in the next two sections.

> *You should read "Adjusting Volume" and related sections in Chapter 9 before starting this next exercise.*

# Setting Volume—No Preamp

Now that you've selected the mic, let's set the volume. This simple case involves using either volume controls on the mic or software controls in OS X to adjust volume.

*We defined the term "unity value" in Chapter 9; it's the setting that neither increases nor decreases volume, like the middle position of Input volume in Figure 11-10.*

**Step 1.** In Sound Preferences, click the Input tab and make sure the correct mic is selected. Then, if it's not there already, set input levels at 50 percent (the middle pip as shown in Figure 11-10). This is the unity value.

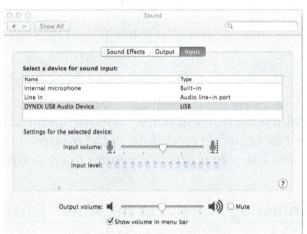

*Figure 11-10. Starting settings in the Sound Preferences pane.*

**Step 2.** Watch the input level shown in Figure 11-10 and speak into the mic at normal volume. If the volume isn't sufficient and the mic has its own volume control, increase mic volume until levels reach the desired targets.

*tip* *As far as I know, there's no way to listen to the incoming audio when using the OS X input level control. You have to record the audio to actually hear the volume. This means you have to trust your meters, record audio or make a test call.*

**Step 3.** If volume is still too low, drag the input volume slider to the right until the volume is in the target range (Figure 11-11).

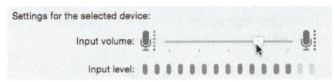

*Figure 11-11. Drag input volume to the right to achieve target levels.*

**Step 4.** Stop talking and check the input level, which should show very little volume. If it shows more, there's noise in the audio. This can be caused by a noisy environment, too much volume boost, or malfunctioning audio gear.

*tip* *If you have a sound editor like GarageBand or Adobe Audition, set levels while recording in the program. You can see the waveform and listen to it after recording to ensure proper volume.*

## Adjusting Volume in the Audio Chain

In Chapter 9, you learned about the audio chain, which is the series of hardware and software products involved in audio production. This can include the mic, preamp, and computer or capture station. Given that all products in the audio chain may have volume and/or gain controls, what's the optimal strategy for adjusting volume?

You learned in Chapter 9 to set volume as early in the chain as possible, which usually is either on the mic or preamp. You want to adjust once and then leave all other volume controls at "unity value," or the setting that neither raises nor lowers volume. That's the high-level concept behind the procedure you're about to follow.

# Setting Volume—With Preamp

That was the simple case; now let's run through the same procedure with a preamp. I'll demonstrate taking the main output from the PreSonus AudioBox 44VSL into the line input on my MacPro.

**Step 1.** In the Sound Preferences Pane, click the Input tab and make sure the correct input is selected (Line in). Then set input levels at the unity value of 50% (the middle pip as shown in Figure 11-12).

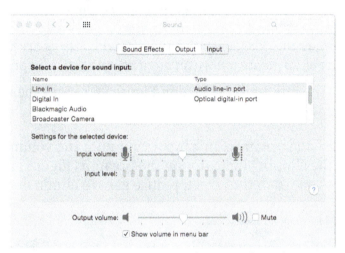

*Figure 11-12. Starting settings in the Sound Preferences pane.*

**Step 2.** On the 44VSL, set input gain to 0, main output to unity value (Figure 11-13). If the mic had gain control, I would set input gain on the preamp to unity value and start by adjusting mic gain.

*As far as I know, there's no way to listen to the incoming audio when using the Mac system input level control. This means you have to trust your meters, record audio or make a test call.*

*Figure 11-13. The PreSonus AudioBox 44VSL with input gain at 0 and Main at unity value. The four knobs on the bottom control gain for the four inputs. Main output controls volume for the main outputs on the back of the unit, while Phones does the same for the headphones. Mixer controls are particular to this model, so please ignore if you're using a different preamp.*

**Step 3.** Watch the input level shown in Figure 11-12 and speak into the mic at normal volume.

**Step 4.** Increase the preamp's mic input gain until the volume is in the target zone. If the clipping indicator on the preamp (Figure 11-13) starts blinking before you reach the target, reduce gain to eliminate clipping.

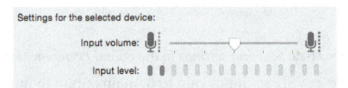

*Figure 11-14. Input levels too low.*

**Step 5.** If peak volumes are too low (Figure 11-14), increase volume using the Main knob on the preamp (Figure 11-13) to achieve the desired target.

**Step 6.** If volume is still too low, drag the input volume slider in Sound Preferences to the right until volume is in the target range (Figure 11-15).

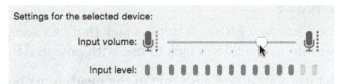

*Figure 11-15. Drag input volume to the right to achieve target levels.*

**Step 7.** Stop talking and check the input level, which should show very little volume—one green bar or less in the microphone volume indicator. If it shows more, there's noise in the audio. This can be caused by a noisy environment, too much volume boost, or malfunctioning audio gear.

*tip If you have a sound editor like GarageBand or Adobe Audition, set levels while recording in the program. You can see the waveform and listen to it after recording to ensure proper volume.*

## What the Heck is a Clipping Indicator?

Most preamps have lights that blink if input volumes exceed a threshold that would produce clipping at the peaks of the audio signal, potentially causing distortion. When adjusting volume with a preamp, you can boost the volume until the light blinks frequently, and then back off until it blinks very infrequently, if at all.

## Key Takeaways

• Most Macs have a TRRS headphone jack that can accept and power an electret mic, and a line in jack to use with powered inputs.

• You can't use a standard TRS mic in the headphone port without a TRS-to-TRRS adapter.

• Many USB-powered mics should work on Macs, as should XLR-to-USB adapters.

• Some conferencing apps allow you to choose and configure audio from within their user interface. When available, use these, because they're typically easier to use and more functional than the default Mac controls.

• When you plug in most mics, OS X will automatically make the new mic the default. The major exception is USB mics.

# Chapter 12: Working with Audio on iOS Devices

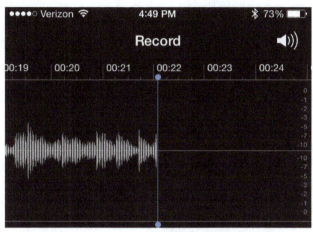

*Figure 12-1. Checking volume in Voice Recorder.*

FaceTime, Skype, and other conferencing tools have greatly expanded the communications capabilities on iOS devices, whether connected via Wi-Fi or 4G. Since you're speaking 2 to 3 feet from the mic, however, audio can be a weak link.

In this chapter, you'll learn how to connect your mic to your iPhone, iPad, or iPod touch, how to select the mic, and how to check volume.

# Overview

The major sections in this chapter cover:

- Understanding the ports on an iOS device

- Connecting mics to an iOS device

- Choosing a mic on an iOS device

- Setting volume on an iOS device (or, more accurately, not setting volume).

Much of the content in this chapter builds on information presented earlier. If you skipped it, I describe what a TRRS plug is in Chapter 7, in a section entitled "A Primer on Connectors." In addition, you can learn about line and mic inputs in the section entitled "A Short Primer on Plugs" in Chapter 7. If you don't know what a TRS-to-TRRS adapter is, go back and read that section.

# iOS Connection Options

There are three connection options for iOS devices: the headphone/mic input port, the Lightning or 30-pin connector, and Bluetooth. Figure 12-2 shows the first two on the iPhone 6. Bluetooth is obviously wireless and has no connector. Let's discuss them in that order.

*Figure 12-2. Audio ports on an iPhone 6.*

## Headphone Jack

You learned about the headphone/mic port back in Chapter 7, but let's review. The plug on all iOS devices is a TRRS port that's functionally identical to the headphone port on MacBooks; It can play stereo audio, accept mono audio input, and supply power to a mic that requires plug-in power.

There's one caveat: for the mic to work, the plug that connects to the headphone port must be identical to the plug on iPhone EarPods shown on the left in Figure 12-3. Actually, it can be your iPhone EarPods, which you can use for conferencing as well as phone calls.

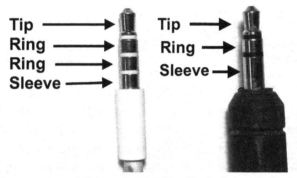

*Figure 12-3. iPhone TRRS EarPod plug on the left,*
*regular mic plug (TRS) on the right.*

However, regular TRS mics, like that shown on the right in Figure 12-3, won't work on an iPhone without an adapter like that shown in Figure 12-4. This adapter has the two critical features needed for a plug for conferencing: it can supply plug-in power to electret mics and it's got a headphone jack out so you can talk as well as listen.

*Figure 12-4. The Azden i-Coustics HX-Mi TRRS adapter.*

Although few users will likely choose to aim this high, as we discussed back in Chapter 7, there are adapters like the IK Multimedia iRig PRE shown in Figure 12-5 that let you connect XLR mics to your iPhone.

*Figure 12-5. The IK Multimedia iRig PRE lets you connect XLR mics to iPhones.*

Installation of the iRig PRE is straightforward: you plug the TRRS connector into the phone as shown in Figure 12-5, and connect the mic to the iRig PRE, which can supply phantom power to the mic if needed. The iRig PRE has gain control for the mic, which is always convenient, as well as a headphone jack, so you can hear what the other person has to say. This isn't a setup I would use for every conference, but if it's worth considering for critical meetings you have to attend on your iPhone.

## Lightning Connector

As discussed in Chapter 7, a growing number of specialty mics connect to the iOS Lightning connector or older 30-pin connector. Unfortunately, while video camera apps do support them, none of the conferencing apps that I tested—including FaceTime, Skype, and Google Hangouts—did.

This doesn't mean that no conference app supports these mics, or that these apps won't support them one day. However, I wouldn't buy a specialty mic for conferencing until I knew that the app I was intending to e did support them.

## Bluetooth Headsets

Bluetooth headsets typically deliver better quality than the internal mic on an iPhone when speaking from FaceTime distance. I find the sound a bit synthetic, but they're unobtrusive and easy enough to use. Each headset has its own pairing mechanism, so you should refer to the headset's instructions to get it up and running before the conference.

# Choosing a Mic on an iOS Device

In the tests I performed, the individual apps recognized and switched over to each new mic as I attached them to the headphone/mic port or turned them on, in the case of Bluetooth. In chapters 13-21 I review app-specific configuration options, so you can get more instruction there.

In general, most apps don't let you manually choose the mic, and some don't even indicate which mic is selected. In these cases, when you have multiple mics connected, the general priority seems to be Bluetooth first, headphone jack next, and embedded mic last. Again, all apps seemed to deploy any new mic once it's attached.

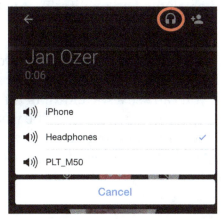

*Figure 12-6. Choosing a mic in Google Hangouts.*

One exception was Google Hangouts, which lets you choose the mic to use and provides feedback as to which mic was in use. This is shown in Figure 12-6, which is an iPhone screen I truncated to save some space. The circled headphones icon on the upper right shows that the mic plugged into the headphone jack is in use. Tap the headphones, and the selection screen appears on the bottom of your screen so you can choose a different mic.

*tip* *If your conferencing app doesn't let you select which mic to use, run the app, disconnect the desired mic, and then reconnect it. The app should select the new mic automatically.*

## Adjusting Mic Volume in iOS

Although there are apps that let you adjust mic volume on the iPhone, none of the conferencing apps that I tested offered this feature. Some do provide volume-related feedback during the call, which I'll discuss in the app-specific chapters, but generally it's too limited to be of any real assistance. The relative lack of volume control and volume-related feedback can be frustrating when you're working with new mics, or even when trying to figure out how the internal mic sounds.

One alternative is try a test call with a friend or colleague and get their feedback regarding audio volume and quality. That will give you the most accurate read.

If that's not an option, connect the new mic and record a few seconds of audio using the Voice Recorder app on the iPhone, or something similar. While you're recording, you can see a waveform in the app that shows the volumes you're producing (Figure 12-7). I describe what a waveform is back in Chapter 9 in the text surrounding Figure 9-2. If you compare the waveform in Figure 12-7 with the examples in Figure 9-2, you'll note that it looks pretty weak, including sub-optimal volumes.

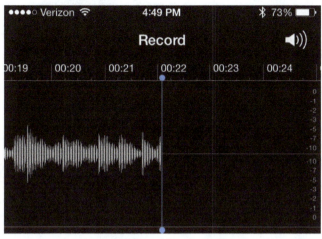

*Figure 12-7. An anemic waveform in the iPhone Voice Recorder app.*

During my tests, the only mic that produced adequate levels was the Shure SM93 connected via the iRig PRE shown in Figure 12-5. Does that mean all the other mics would produce audio too low to understand at the other end?

Not necessarily. There's a technology called "automatic gain control," or AGC, that app developers can apply to make your audio more usable. For example, if the audio volume is too low, AGC can automatically boost it to more audible levels and you wouldn't necessarily know it.

That's what appeared to happen when I recorded several calls on my Mac Pro, which I made from my iPhone using Skype and Google Hangouts. Although the iRig PRE/SM93 produced the highest volume, the differential was much less than what I was seeing in the Voice Recorder app, so AGC was probably kicking in to boost the volume.

Of course, AGC comes at a price. Boosting volume in software introduces noise into the audio, which is never good. So you should definitely look for a mic that produces strong volumes in Voice Recorder. I just don't want you to panic if your EarPods or Bluetooth headset don't appear to produce sufficient levels in that app, because odds are good that AGC will increase the volume to acceptable levels when you're actually participating in a FaceTime, Skype, or Google Hangouts conference.

*tip* *If you're really concerned about mic volume, try making a test call with Skype. You'll get to hear exactly how you sound to a remote listener. I describe how in Chapter 19.*

## Audio Processing in iOS

There's a lot going on behind the scenes with voice calls and presumably conferencing apps, according to the Nethervoice website (bit.ly/iOS_voice). This includes automatic gain control, a high-pass audio filter that minimizes plosives (pops on Bs and Ps), and noise reduction. These make your voice more distinct, but slightly artificial.

None of the conferencing apps I reviewed let you to disable this processing, which is probably for the best. If you're recording audio, however, you probably should disable these effects, which you can in some recording programs. There's an amazing demo of how much better audio sounds without AGC at bit.ly/ACG_off. If you're interested in recording audio on your iOS device, you should definitely give it a listen.

# Key Takeaways

• The headphone jack on your iOS device is a TRRS plug, which can accept mic input from the EarPods that came with your device.

• You can't use a standard TRS mic without an adapter.

• If you buy an adapter, make sure it can supply plug-in power to your electret mics and that it has a headphone jack.

• Bluetooth devices typically produce better quality than the embedded mic on the iPhone, as will an external mic.

• As of May 2015, none of the conferencing apps I tested recognize mics that connect via the Lightning or 30-pin connector.

• Most iOS devices seem to switch to any mic installed once they are running. Otherwise, they seem to prioritize Bluetooth mics (if any), then mics installed on the headset port, and then the internal mic.

• Very few conferencing apps let you manually choose which mic to use, but if you disconnect the desired mic and then reconnect it when the program is running, it should select it automatically.

• No conference apps let you adjust mic volume. You'll have to test beforehand to make sure your mic is producing adequate volume.

• Most conferencing apps use automatic gain control (AGC) to ensure the audio you're transmitting has adequate volume.

# Chapter 13: Working with Audio on Android Devices

*Figure 13-1. Choosing a mic in Google Hangouts. If only it were so easy in other programs.*

The mics in most Android phones work well for voice calls, but can be faint and noisy when used for Skype or Google Hangouts videoconferences. Ditto for the mics in Android tablets.

In this chapter, you'll learn how to connect an external mic to your Android device, how to select the mic, and how to check volume.

# Overview

The major sections in this chapter cover:

- Understanding the ports on an Android device

- Connecting mics to an Android device

- Choosing a mic on an Android device

- Setting volume on an Android device (or, more appropriately, not setting volume).

Much of the content in this chapter builds on information presented earlier. If you skipped it, I describe what a TRRS plug is in Chapter 7, in a section entitled "A Primer on Connectors." In addition, you can learn about line and mic inputs in the section entitled "A Short Primer on Plugs" in Chapter 7. If you don't know what a TRS-to-TRRS adapter is, go back and read that section.

# Android Connection Options

There are three connection options for Android devices: the headphone/ mic input port, the USB connector, and Bluetooth. Figure 13-2 shows the first two on my Samsung Galaxy Nexus 10 tablet. As mentioned in Chapter 7, none of the current USB mics work in Skype and Google Hangouts, so I won't discuss USB mics any further. Bluetooth isn't shown, of course, because it's wireless and there is no connector.

*Figure 13-2. Audio ports on a Samsung Galaxy Nexus 10.*

## Headphone Jack

You learned about the headphone/mic port back in Chapter 7, but let's review. The plug on all Android devices is a TRRS port that's functionally identical to the headphone port on MacBooks. It can play stereo audio, accept mono audio input, and supply power to a mic that requires plug-in power.

The only caveat is that the plug inserted into this port must be identical to the plug on Samsung headset shown on the left in Figure 13-3. Actually, it can be your Samsung headset, which can serve as both mic and headset.

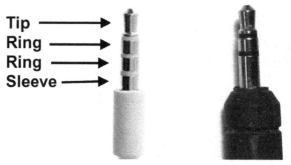

*Figure 13-3. Samsung headset TRRS plug on the left,*
*regular mic plug (TRS) on the right.*

However, this also means that regular TRS mics, like that shown on the right in Figure 13-3, won't work on most Android devices without an adapter like that shown in Figure 13-4. This adapter has the two critical features needed for a plug for conferencing: it can supply plug-in power to electret mics and it has a headphone jack out so you can talk as well as listen.

*Figure 13-4. The Azden i-Coustics HX-Mi TRRS adapter.*

Although few users will likely choose to aim this high, as we discussed back in Chapter 7, there are adapters like the IK Multimedia iRig PRE shown in Figure 13-5 that let you connect XLR mics to your Android device.

*Figure 13-5. The IK Multimedia iRig PRE lets you connect XLR mics to Android devices.*

Installation of the iRig PRE is straightforward: you plug the TRRS connector into the phone as shown in Figure 12-5, and connect the mic to the iRig PRE, which can supply phantom power to the mic if needed. The iRig PRE has gain control for the mic, which is always convenient, as well as a headphone jack, so you can hear what the other person has to say. This isn't a setup I would use for every conference, but if it's worth considering for critical meetings you have to attend on your Android device.

⚠ *Caution! As I mentioned back in Chapter 7, there are two incompatible TRRS standards: one used by Apple, the other used by some older Android devices. While most headsets and adapters designed for Apple iOS devices should work with Android devices, there may be some older Android devices that won't be compatible.*

## Bluetooth Headsets

Bluetooth headsets are another option that typically deliver better quality than the internal mic on an Android device when speaking from Skype video call distance. I find the sound a bit synthetic, but they're unobtrusive and easy enough to use. Each headset has its own pairing mechanism, so you should refer to the product instructions to get it up and running before the conference.

# Choosing a Mic on Your Android Device

For the most part, the apps I tested performed as follows:

- If a Bluetooth mic was installed when the program was loaded, it would use that mic, even if there was a mic in the headphone port.

- If the Bluetooth mic was turned on after the application loaded, sometimes it was recognized sometimes not.

- If the Bluetooth mic was shut off during the call, the app would automatically fall over to a mic in the headphone port, if present, or the on-device mic.

- If you inserted a mic into the headphone jack during the call, the app would recognize the mic.

- If you removed the mic from the headphone jack during the call, it would fall over to the on-device mic.

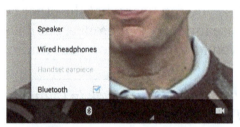

*Figure 13-6. Choosing a mic in Google Hangouts.*

The bottom line is that if you want to use your Bluetooth mic, have it set up and running before you run the program. If you're running Google Hangouts, you can manually switch to the mic at any time. With Skype, the only other program I tried on Android, you could not. Chapter 19 covers the audio/visual aspects of running Skype on Android (as well as iOS, Mac and Windows), while Chapter 15 does the same for Google Hangouts.

# Adjusting Mic Volume in Android

None of the conferencing apps I tested offered the ability to adjust mic volume, and there was precious little feedback regarding audio volume in the application. This makes it tough to work with external mics, or even figure out if the internal mic is generating sufficient volume.

The best alternative is a test call with a friend to get their feedback regarding volume and quality.

One free app I used in my testing was Decibel-O-Meter (Figure 13-7), which loads and continuously displays mic input volume in decibels. This was great for figuring out which mic was active and for assessing mic volume before conferencing.

*Figure 13-7. The aptly named Decibel-O-Meter.*

There are also numerous Android apps, free and otherwise, that you can use to record audio and listen to the recording to gauge volume. If recording volume sounds really low during testing, or looks weak on the Decibel-O-Meter, don't despair. That's because most Android conferencing apps deploy a technology called "automatic gain control", or AGC, that app developers can apply to make your audio more usable. For example, if the audio volume is too low, the software can boost it to more audible levels behind the scenes and you wouldn't necessarily know it.

Of course, AGC comes at a price. Boosting volume adds noise into the audio, which is never good. So you should definitely look for a mic that produces strong volumes in whatever recording app you use. I just don't want you to panic if your headset or mic don't appear to produce sufficient levels in that app, because odds are good that AGC will increase the volume to acceptable levels when you're participating in a Skype or Google Hangouts conference.

If producing sufficient volume is a problem, the best option is a preamp like the IK Multimedia iRig PRE shown in Figure 13-5, connected to a good XLR mic. It's a bit of a pain to set up, but the iRig's volume control will help make sure that you produce sufficient volume without engaging Android's AGC.

*If you're really concerned about mic volume, try making a test call with Skype. You'll get to hear exactly how you sound to a remote listener. I describe how in Chapter 19.*

## Audio Effects in Android

Here's the definition of Automatic Gain Control (AGC) from the Android Developers reference.

> Automatic Gain Control (AGC) is an audio pre-processing which automatically normalizes the output of the captured signal by boosting or lowering input from the microphone to match a preset level so that the output signal level is virtually constant. AGC can be used by applications where the input signal dynamic range is not important but where a constant strong capture level is desired.

The Android OS makes it simple to deploy other technologies like noise suppression and echo cancellation, which improve call clarity, but can make your voice sound slightly synthetic (bit.ly/Android_voice). None of the conferencing apps I tested let you disable any of these technologies, although some recording apps may.

# Key Takeaways

• The headphone jack on your Android device is a TRRS plug that can accept mic input from the headset that came with your device.

• You can't use a standard TRS mic without an adapter.

• If you buy an adapter, make sure it can supply plug-in power to your electret mics and that it has a headphone jack.

• Bluetooth devices may produce better quality than the embedded mic on your Android device, as will an external mic.

◇As of May 2015, none of the conferencing apps I tested recognize mics that connect via the USB port.

• Most Android devices seem to switch to any mic installed once they are running. Otherwise, they seem to prioritize Bluetooth mics (if any), then mics installed on the headset port, and then the internal mic.

• No conference apps let you adjust mic volume. You'll have to test beforehand to make sure your mic is producing adequate volume.

• Most conferencing apps use automatic gain control (AGC) to ensure the audio you're transmitting has adequate volume.

# Chapter 14: Working with FaceTime

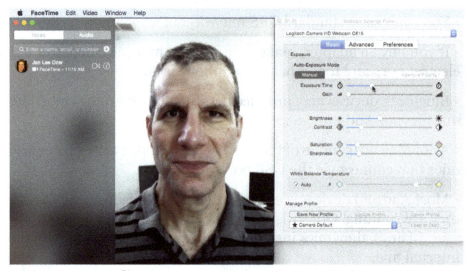

*Figure 14-1. Adjusting exposure in Mactaris Webcam Settings.*

FaceTime is Apple's videoconferencing application, which is available on all recent iOS devices and on the Mac, but not on Android or Windows. Perhaps for this reason, most business users tend to prefer Skype, which is available on all four platforms and more.

In this chapter, I'll describe the available options for optimizing FaceTime's audio/video settings. This is the shortest chapter in the book—your hint that there aren't many options.

# Overview

You learned how to optimize your webcam settings for the Mac and iOS in Chapter 6, and how to work with audio on the Mac and on iOS devices in Chapters 11 and 12, respectively. These chapters were for general applications; here we'll look at these operations for FaceTime.

In this chapter, I'm going to presume that you at least skimmed the aforementioned chapters; while there will be some duplication, I'm not going to completely reinvent the wheel.

This chapter is not meant to be a general primer on FaceTime operation. Rather, you'll learn how to optimize A/V settings for FaceTime on the Mac and iOS platforms. Specifically, you will learn:

- How to optimize video settings for FaceTime on the Mac

- How to choose a mic and adjust volume for FaceTime on the Mac

- How to optimize video settings for FaceTime on iOS devices

- How to choose a mic and adjust volume for FaceTime on iOS devices.

Let's get started.

# FaceTime on the Mac

Apple made FaceTime on the Mac as minimalistic as possible, with no controls for adjusting webcam settings and no integrated volume controls. You can address the former with a third-party program like Mactaris Webcam Settings, which is shown on the right in Figure 14-1. You can adjust mic and speaker volume using the general procedures you learned back in Chapter 11.

## Choosing a Webcam

If you have multiple webcams, choose the desired webcam by selecting Video and then the desired webcam (Figure 14-2)

*Figure 14-2. Choosing the webcam.*

## Optimizing Your Webcam Settings

After selecting the webcam, there's at least a chance you'll want to optimize the settings. In this case, I recommend Webcam Settings from Mactaris, which you can read about at bit.ly/web_set. Here's a close-up view of the main Webcam Setting controls (Figure 14-3).

*Figure 14-3. The primary controls in the Webcam Settings program.*

Your controls will vary by webcam and program. I presented a structured workflow for optimizing these settings (luminance, then color, then sharpness) back in Chapter 6 in a section entitled "Optimizing Your Webcam Settings."

## Choosing a Microphone in FaceTime

If you have multiple mics installed, choose the desired mic by selecting Video and then the desired mic (Figure 14-4). As you learned back in Chapter 6, the AudioBox 44VSL is a pre-amp from PreSonus that I frequently pair with the Shure SM93 lavalier mic for conferences and webinars.

*Figure 14-4. Choosing the desired mic in FaceTime.*

## Adjusting Mic Volume

After choosing the mic, you adjust volume in the Sound Preferences (Figure 14-5). You can learn how to open Sound Preferences in a section entitled "Choosing a Mic in OS X" in Chapter 11, specifically Figure 11-7 (or press the Option key and click the sound icon in the menu bar). The next two sections in that chapter cover setting volume. As a precursor, to learn how to set the appropriate volume, you might want to read Chapter 9— particularly the section entitled "Adjusting Volume."

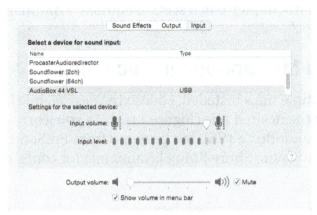

*Figure 14-5. Adjusting volume in Sound Preferences.*

So there you have it. Now you've got the inside skinny on controlling audio and video for FaceTime on the Mac. Let's switch over to FaceTime for iOS devices.

*Apple has a short and useful tutorial on setting up FaceTime on iOS at bit.ly/IOS_FT.*

# FaceTime on iOS

While computers are computers, with all the inherent configurability and complexity thereof, iPhones and iPads are consumer electronics devices, designed to be operated by completely unsophisticated users. As such, FaceTime has very few user-configurable options, whether within FaceTime, in the iOS operating system or via third-party apps.

Regarding the webcam, obviously there's only one, so you don't need to choose it. As far as I'm aware, there are no webcam configuration options for exposure or white balance controls on the iPhone. This makes lighting extremely important when making video calls via FaceTime. Check Chapter 5 for simple, inexpensive techniques you can use to ensure the best possible lighting.

*tip* *To shoot in landscape mode with FaceTime, turn your iPhone sideways. The program will automatically adjust on your phone and on the recipient's device.*

## Choosing the Mic in FaceTime

To choose a mic in FaceTime, press the mic icon on the bottom of the screen—the icon on the right in Figure 14-6. If the controls aren't showing, simply tap the screen.

*Figure 14-6. Click the button on the right to select a mic.*

This brings up the menu shown in Figure 14-7. Click the mic you want to use, and then Hide, and FaceTime will switch over to the selected mic.

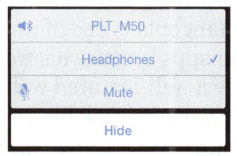

*Figure 14-7. Choosing the desired mic.*

There is no way to adjust mic volume, although most conferencing apps use automatic gain control (AGC) to ensure adequate volume. If you really want to optimize the volume of your calls, consider a preamp with gain control, like the IK Multimedia iRig PRE shown back in Figure 12-5. You can find a discussion of your other mic options in Chapter 12 in the section entitled "Adjusting Mic Volume in iOS."

# Chapter 15: Working with Google Hangouts

*Figure 15-1. Writing is a solitary profession; I had to call myself to get this screenshot.*

Google Hangouts is one of my favorite conferencing apps because it's free and it lets me produce a well-featured webinar that's immediately made available on YouTube.

In this chapter, I'll detail audio and video operation for Google Hangouts in Windows, on the Mac, and on iOS and Android mobile platforms.

# Overview

This chapter is not meant to be a general primer on Google Hangouts operation. Rather, I focus on how to optimize video and audio quality when using Google Hangouts in Windows 7, on the Mac, and on iOS and Android mobile devices. Specifically, in this chapter, you will learn:

- How to optimize video and audio settings for Google Hangouts in Windows 7

- How to optimize video and audio settings for Google Hangouts on the Mac

- How to optimize video and audio settings for Google Hangouts on iOS devices

- How to optimize video and audio settings for Google Hangouts on Android devices.

Note that Google Hangouts is a plug-in or app that's not loaded natively on any of the discussed platforms. You should download and install the app or plug-in before getting started.

As a caveat, Google Hangouts is a fast-moving application, and mobile apps, in particular, are in a constant state of flux. I apologize in advance if the Google Hangouts app or plug-in you're using differs significantly from what's shown here. Please contact me at jan@thewebcambook.com for any particularly egregious errors or omissions, or contact me through www.thewebcambook.com.

# Google Hangouts on Windows

I'll demonstrate on Windows 7, since it still has the dominant share of Windows users. I'll demonstrate using Google Chrome with the Hangouts extension installed and enabled, which is the recommended configuration.

If you're working in Chrome without the extension or in other browsers, I can't guarantee that you'll see the same screens that I'll show below.

Note that while you can choose a webcam and mic within the Google Hangout interface, you can't adjust the webcam settings or audio volume within that interface. For the webcam, you'll have to optimize your settings before you start your hangout, because you probably won't be able to access your webcam controls once the webcam is being used in Google Hangouts. You will be able to adjust audio volume using the standard Windows controls during the call. I'll remind you where to find the webcam and volume controls in the respective sections below.

## Choosing the Webcam

**Step 1.** In the toolbar atop the Google Hangouts interface, click the Settings icon (Figure 15-2). The Google Hangouts Settings window opens.

*Figure 15-2. Open the Google Hangout Settings window.*

**Step 2.** In the Settings window, click the Webcam drop-down list and choose the desired webcam (Figure 15-3).

*Figure 15-3. Choose the desired webcam in the Webcam drop-down list.*

## Optimizing Video Settings

As mentioned above, you can't access your webcam's optimization controls from within the Google Hangouts app. This means you'll have to make sure your webcam settings are optimized before you start your Google Hangout. Unfortunately, these settings are not located in the same application for all webcams; for example, on my HP notebook, they're located in the HP Webcam program. So job number 1 is to find the webcam application, which will probably look something like Figure 15-4, but not exactly like the figure unless you have the exact same notebook.

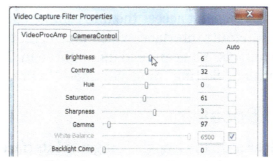

*Figure 15-4. The Video Capture Filter Properties window.*

Once you find the webcam app, refer back to the structured workflow for optimizing these settings (luminance, then color, then sharpness) in Chapter 6 in a section entitled "Optimizing Your Webcam Settings."

## Choosing the Mic

**Step 1.** In the toolbar atop the Google Hangouts interface, click the Settings icon (Figure 15-2). The Google Hangouts Settings window opens.

**Step 2.** In the Settings window, click the Microphone drop-down list and choose the desired mic (Figure 15-5).

*Figure 15-5. Choosing the desired mic.*

## Adjusting Mic Volume

As mentioned above, you can't access the mic volume controls from within the Google Hangouts interface, which means that you'll have to use Windows general controls. You can read up on these in Chapter 10, starting with the section entitled "Setting Input Volume—No Preamp."

## Choosing the Speaker

**Step 1.** In the toolbar atop the Google Hangouts interface, click the Settings icon (Figure 15-2). The Google Hangouts Settings window opens.

**Step 2.** In the Settings window, click the Speakers drop-down list and choose the desired speaker or output (Figure 15-6).

*Figure 15-6. Choosing the desired speaker.*

Set the speaker volume using the normal speaker control on the bottom right of the Windows toolbar.

# Google Hangouts on the Mac

I'll demonstrate using Google Chrome with the Hangouts extension installed and enabled, which is the recommended configuration. If you're working in Chrome without the extension or in other browsers, I can't guarantee that you'll see the same screens I'll show below.

Note that while you can choose a webcam and mic within the Google Hangout interface, you can't adjust the webcam settings or audio volume within that interface. For the webcam, you can use a third-party program like Mactaris Webcam Settings, which I'll show you below. For audio, you'll have to use the typical Mac controls, which I'll show you as well.

## Choosing the Webcam

**Step 1.** In the toolbar atop the Google Hangouts interface, click the Settings icon (Figure 15-7). The Google Hangouts Settings window opens.

*Figure 15-7. Opening the Google Hangout Settings window.*

**Step 2.** In the Settings window, click the Webcam drop-down list and choose the desired webcam (Figure 15-8).

*Figure 15-8. Choose the desired webcam in the Webcam drop-down list.*

## Optimizing Your Webcam Settings

As mentioned, the Google Hangouts interface doesn't include any webcam optimizations. If you need to adjust brightness, color, or sharpness, try Webcam Settings from Mactaris ([bit.ly/web_set](bit.ly/web_set)). Here's a close-up view of the main Webcam Setting controls (Figure 15-9).

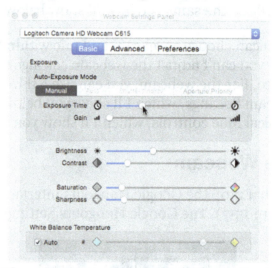

*Figure 15-9. The primary controls in the Webcam Settings program.*

If you use Webcam Settings or another program, your controls will vary by webcam and program. I preset a structured workflow for optimizing these settings (luminance, then color, then sharpness) back in Chapter 6 in a section entitled "Optimizing Your Webcam Settings."

## Choosing the Mic

**Step 1.** In the toolbar atop the Google Hangouts interface, click the Settings icon (Figure 15-7). The Google Hangouts Settings window opens.

**Step 2.** In the Settings window, click the Microphone drop-down list and choose the desired mic (Figure 15-10).

*Figure 15-10. Choosing the desired mic.*

## Adjusting Mic Volume

After choosing the mic, you adjust volume in the Sound Preferences (Figure 15-11). You can learn how to open Sound Preferences in a section entitled "Choosing a Mic in OS X" in Chapter 11, specifically Figure 11-7 (or press the Option key and click the sound icon in the menu bar to open Sound Preferences). The next two sections in that chapter cover setting volume. As a precursor, to learn how to set the appropriate volume, you might want to read Chapter 9—particularly the section entitled "Adjusting Volume."

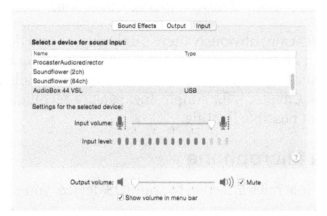

*Figure 15-11. Adjusting volume in Sound Preferences.*

## Choosing the Speaker

**Step 1.** In the toolbar atop the Google Hangouts interface, click the Settings icon (Figure 15-7). The Google Hangouts Settings window opens.

**Step 2.** In the Settings window, click the Speakers drop-down list and choose the desired speaker or output (Figure 15-12).

*Figure 15-12. Choosing the desired speaker.*

Set volume using the speaker control on the right of the top Mac menu bar.

# Google Hangouts on iOS

On the iOS platform, Google Hangouts has very few user-configurable options, whether within Hangouts, in the iOS operating system, or via third-party apps. I'm demonstrating operation from an iPhone 6, which should be similar, but not identical, to iPad operation.

Regarding the webcam, obviously there's only one, so you don't need to choose it. I found no exposure or white balance controls on the iPhone or iPad. This makes lighting critical when making video calls via Google Hangouts. Check Chapter 5 for simple, inexpensive techniques you can use to ensure the best possible lighting.

## Choosing a Microphone

If you have multiple mics attached to your iOS device, you can select the desired mic. Follow this procedure.

**Step 1.** Once in the call, on the top toolbar, click the second icon from the right (Figure 15-13). The mic selection screen opens (Figure 15-14).

*Figure 15-13. The call toolbar. The second icon from the right is for the mic; the first is for switching cameras from front to back.*

**Step 2.** Choose the desired mic (Figure 15-14), and then choose Hide to close the mic selection screen.

*Figure 15-14. Choosing the desired mic.*

There is no way to adjust mic volume from within the interface, although Google Hangouts seems to use automatic gain control (AGC) to ensure adequate volume. If you really want to optimize the volume of your calls, consider a preamp with gain control, like the IK Multimedia iRig PRE shown in Figure 12-5. You can learn how to test mic volume in Chapter 12 in the section "Adjusting Mic Volume in iOS."

Google Hangouts will switch to a headphone once it's plugged in, and switch back to the internal speaker once it's removed. Use the hardware volume controls on the mobile device to adjust output volume.

## Google Hangouts on Android

On Android, Google Hangouts has few user-configurable options, whether within Google Hangouts, in the Android operating system, or via third-party apps. I'm demonstrating operation on a Samsung Galaxy Nexus 10, which should be similar, but not identical, to Android smartphone operation.

Regarding the webcam, obviously there's only one, so you don't need to choose it. I found no exposure or white balance controls on the tablet. This makes lighting extremely important when making video calls via Google Hangouts. Check Chapter 5 for simple, inexpensive techniques you can use to ensure the best possible lighting.

## Choosing a Mic

If you have multiple mics attached to your Android device, you can select the desired mic. Follow this procedure.

**Step 1.** Once in the call, on the bottom toolbar, click the second icon from the left (Figure 15-15). The mic selection screen opens (Figure 15-16).

*Figure 15-15. The call toolbar. The second icon from the left is for the mic; the one on the far right is for switching cameras from front to back.*

**Step 2.** Choose the desired mic (Figure 15-16), and then press anywhere on the screen to close the mic selection screen.

*Figure 15-16. Choosing the desired mic.*

There is no way to adjust mic volume from within the interface, although Google Hangouts seems to use automatic gain control (AGC) to ensure adequate volume. If you really want to optimize the volume of your calls, consider a preamp with gain control, like the IK Multimedia iRig PRE shown in Figure 13-5. You can learn how to test mic volume in Chapter 13 in the section entitled "Adjusting Mic Volume in Android."

Google Hangouts will switch to any headphone once you plug it in, and switch back to the internal speaker once it's removed. Use the hardware volume controls on the mobile device to adjust output volume.

# Chapter 16: Working with GoToWebinar

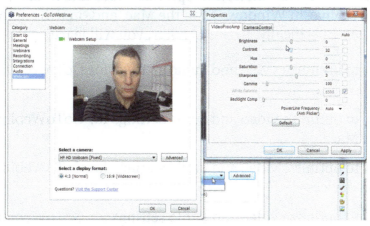

*Figure 16-1. Configuring the GoToWebinar webcam in Windows.*

GoToWebinar and GoToMeeting are sister services provided by Citrix Systems. Although I'll demonstrate using controls from GoToWebinar, the audio/video configuration options shown should work identically in GoToMeeting.

Specifically, in this chapter, I'll detail how to configure audio and video for GoToWebinar in Windows, on the Mac, and on iOS and Android mobile platforms.

# Overview

This chapter is not meant to be a general primer on GoToWebinar operation. Rather, I focus on how to optimize video and audio quality when using GoToWebinar in Windows 7, on the Mac, and on iOS and Android mobile devices. Specifically, in this chapter, you will learn:

• How to optimize video and audio settings for GoToWebinar in Windows 7

• How to optimize video and audio settings for GoToWebinar on the Mac

• How to optimize video and audio settings for GoToWebinar on iOS devices

• How to optimize video and audio settings for GoToWebinar on Android devices.

Note that GoToWebinar is a plug-in or app that's not loaded natively on any of the discussed platforms. You should download and install the app or plug-in before getting started.

As a caveat, GoToWebinar is a fast-moving application, and mobile apps, in particular, are in a constant state of flux. I apologize in advance if the GoToWebinar app or plug-in you're using differs significantly from what's shown here. Please contact me at jan@thewebcambook.com for any particularly egregious errors or omissions, or contact me through www.thewebcambook.com.

# GoToWebinar on Windows 7

I'll demonstrate on Windows 7, since it still has the dominant share of Windows users. I'll demonstrate using Google Chrome with the GoToWebinar extension installed and enabled. If you're working in a different browser, you should see the same screens as shown below, but I can't guarantee it.

## Choosing the Webcam

If you have multiple webcams installed on your computer—virtual or real—you may have to choose the desired webcam before getting started. Here's how to do that. Note that you must enable video in the meeting or conference first to see these screens.

**Step 1.** On the top left of the GoToWebinar Viewer interface, click Webcams and choose Preferences on the bottom of the menu (Figure 16-2). The GoToWebinar Preferences window opens with the Webcams tab selected.

*Figure 16-2. Opening the GoToWebinar Preferences window.*

**Step 2.** In GoToWebinar Preferences, click the Select a camera drop-down list and choose the desired webcam (Figure 16-3). Click OK to close the dialog, or leave it open to customize the webcam configuration.

*Figure 16-3. Choose the desired webcam in the Select a camera drop-down list.*

*tip* You can access GoToWebinar Preferences by right-clicking the GoToWebinar daisy icon in the system tray and choosing Preferences.

## Optimizing Video Settings

**Step 1.** In GoToWebinar Preferences (Figure 16-3), choose between a 4:3 or 16:9 aspect ratio. The latter looks cooler, but unless there's more than one subject in the camera, 4:3 is probably most efficient.

**Step 2.** In GoToWebinar Preferences (Figure 16-3), click the Advanced button to the right of the Select a camera drop-down list. GoToWebinar opens the Properties dialog for your Webcam (on the right in Figure 16-4).

**Step 3.** When you're done configuring, click OK to close the Properties dialog, and OK again to close the Preferences window.

I presented a structured workflow for optimizing these settings (luminance, then color, then sharpness) back in Chapter 6 in a section entitled "Optimizing Your Webcam Settings." Refer back to that section when adjusting these settings.

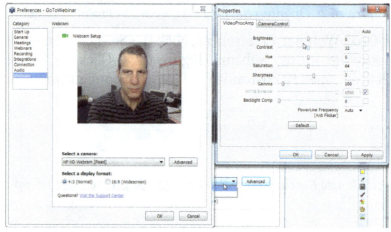

*Figure 16-4. The webcam configuration window.*

*tip* *The name of the window that opens when you click the Advanced button in Figure 16-3 will likely be different from that shown in Figure 16-4, and the controls will be different depending on your webcam. Refer back to Chapter 6 to learn how to optimize these controls.*

## Choosing the Mic and Adjusting Volume

In GoToWebinar, if you use computer for audio, you can choose a mic and speakers, and set volume. Here's how.

**Step 1.** On the top left of the GoToWebinar Viewer interface, click Webcams and choose Preferences on the bottom of the menu (Figure 16-2). The GoToWebinar Preferences window opens with Webcam selected. Click the Audio selection on the left to open Audio preferences (Figure 16-5).

*Figure 16-5. Selecting the Audio tab in GoToWebinar Preferences.*

**Step 2.** In the Audio Preferences window, click the Microphone drop-down list and choose the desired mic (Figure 16-6).

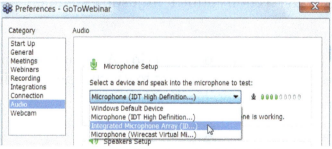

*Figure 16-6. Choosing the desired mic.*

***Step 3.*** Beneath the Microphone drop-down list, configure the Advanced Settings (Figure 16-7).

   • Select the Automatically adjust my system mixer settings checkbox to let GoToWebinar control mic volume. This is the default configuration and works well. If you notice volume increasing when you're quiet (so essentially, the noise gets louder), you may want to deselect this. If you do, you'll have to control audio using Windows' controls, which you can learn how to do in Chapter 10.

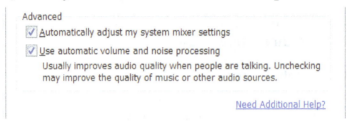

*Figure 16-7. Configuring GoToWebinar's Advanced audio settings.*

   • Select the Use automatic volume and noise processing, which (as the dialog states) usually improves speech but may degrade music. I would leave this checked unless you hear distortion in your audio, in which case I would deselect.

***Step 4.*** Click OK to close the dialog (or leave open to choose the Speaker in the next step).

To learn how to set the appropriate volume, read Chapter 9—particularly the section entitled "Adjusting Volume."

If you add a mic during a GoToWebinar session in Windows, GoToWebinar will ask if you want to use that mic, which simplifies adding a mic mid-conference.

## Choosing the Speakers and Adjusting Volume

**Step 1.** Follow the steps in the previous exercise to open GoToWebinar Preferences and select the Audio tab. In the Speakers Setup drop-down list, choose the desired speakers (top of Figure 16-8).

**Step 2.** Click the Play Sound button to play the test sounds, and drag the volume slider to the desired level.

**Step 3.** Click Stop Sound to Stop the audio.

*Figure 16-8. Choosing the desired speaker and setting speaker volume.*

**Step 4.** Click OK to close the GoToWebinar Preferences.

*Note that the GoToWebinar help file recommends using a USB headset for audio and video. So you should have one handy in case echo starts to be a problem on your call.*

# GoToWebinar on the Mac

On the Mac, you choose your webcam within the GoToWebinar interface, but optimize video quality outside the plug-in. For audio, you can choose mic and speaker and set volume for both inside the plug-in.

## Choosing the Webcam

If you have multiple webcams installed on your computer—virtual or real—you may have to choose the desired webcam before getting started.

Here's how to do that. Note that you must enable video in the meeting or conference first to see these screens.

**Step 1.** On the top left of the GoToWebinar Viewer interface, click Webcams and choose Preferences on the bottom of the menu (Figure 16-9). The GoToWebinar Preferences window opens with the Webcam tab selected.

*Figure 16-9. Opening the GoToWebinar Preferences window.*

**Step 2.** In GoToWebinar Preferences, click the Select a camera drop-down list and choose the desired webcam (Figure 16-10). Click OK to close the dialog, or leave it open to customize the webcam configuration.

*Figure 16-10. Choose the desired webcam in the Select a camera drop-down list.*

> *Since GoToWebinar can choose the Blackmagic capture device in my Mac Pro, it may recognize a camera attached to the card, a nice higher-quality option when a webcam won't do. See the final section in Chapter 2, "Going Beyond the Webcam," for further discussion of this. Also see the article at bit.ly/HDCAM_MacWebcam, which discusses this precise issue.*

## Optimizing Your Webcam Settings

As mentioned, the GoToWebinar Mac interface doesn't include any webcam optimizations, or at least doesn't seem to on any of the Macs I've used or tested. If you need to adjust brightness, color, or sharpness, I recommend Webcam Settings from Mactaris, which you can read about at [bit.ly/web_set](bit.ly/web_set). Here's a close-up view of the main Webcam Setting controls (Figure 16-11), where I'm using these controls to configure the webcam on my Mac Pro.

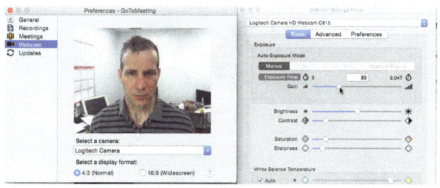

*Figure 16-11. Configuring the webcam with the Webcam Settings program.*

If you use Webcam Settings or another program, your controls will vary by webcam and program. I presented a structured workflow for optimizing these settings (luminance, then color, then sharpness) back in Chapter 6 in a section entitled "Optimizing Your Webcam Settings."

## Choosing the Mic and Adjusting Volume

In GoToWebinar on the Mac, you choose your mic in the Audio pane of the Control Panel, but adjust volume using OS X controls that you learned back in Chapter 11. Here's how.

**Step 1.** In the Audio pane of the control panel, click the mic icon and choose the desired mic (Figure 16-12).

*Figure 16-12. Choosing the desired mic.*

**Step 2.** To open Sound Preferences to adjust input volume, press the Option key and click the sound icon in the menu bar on the upper right. Scroll down and choose Sound Preferences (Figure 16-13). OS X opens Sound Preferences, open to the Output tab.

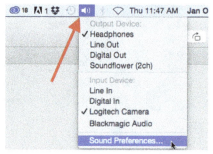

*Figure 16-13. Opening Sound Preferences dialog.*

**Step 3.** In Sound Preferences, (Figure 16-14), click the Input tab on top to view the Input settings, and confirm that the desired mic is selected.

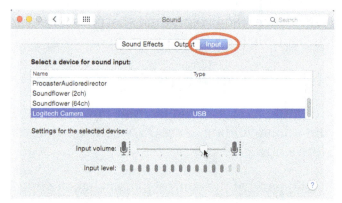

*Figure 16-14. Drag the Input volume to the desired level.*

**Step 4.** In Sound Preferences, drag the input volume slider until the volume is in the target range (Figure 16-14). The technique used will vary based upon whether you are using a preamp or not, and both are covered in Chapter 11 in sections entitled "Setting Volumes—No Preamp," and "Setting Volumes—With Preamp." For a general discussion of target volume, see the section "What's the Target Volume?" in Chapter 9.

**Step 5.** You can close Sound Preferences, or leave it open so you can adjust input volume during the conference.

# Choosing the Speakers and Adjusting Volume

As with mic selection and configuration, you choose the speaker in the Audio pane and adjust volume using OS X system controls.

**Step 1.** In the Audio pane of the control panel, click the speakers icon and choose the desired speakers (Figure 16-15).

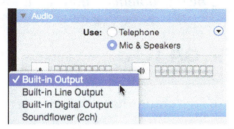

*Figure 16-15. Choosing the desired speakers.*

**Step 2.** To open Sound Preferences to adjust output volume, press the Option key and click the sound icon in the menu bar on the upper right. Scroll down and choose Sound Preferences (Figure 16-13). OS X opens the Sound Preferences, open to the Output tab.

**Step 3.** Once Sound Preferences is open, confirm that the desired output is selected (Figure 16-16).

*Figure 16-16. Drag the Output volume to the desired level.*

**Step 4.** Drag the Output volume to the desired level.

**Step 5.** You can close Sound Preferences, or leave it open so you can adjust output volume during the conference.

*tip* *Note that the GoToWebinar help file recommends using a USB headset for audio and video. So you should have one handy in case echo starts to be a problem on your call.*

# GoToWebinar on iOS

On the iOS platform, GoToWebinar has very few user-configurable options, whether within GoToWebinar, in the iOS operating system, or via third-party apps. Regarding the webcam, you can switch between front and back cameras, but otherwise, there are no webcam configurations for exposure or white balance controls. This makes lighting critical when making video calls via GoToWebinar on this platform. Check Chapter 5 for simple, inexpensive techniques you can use to ensure the best possible lighting.

## Choosing the Mic

There's no mic selection option in GoToWebinar. If you have multiple mics attached to your iOS device, GoToWebinar seems to use the last mic you added, but it's hard to be sure this works in every instance. If you add a mic during a call, GoToWebinar uses that mic. If you remove the mic—say, by shutting off your Bluetooth device—GoToWebinar automatically transitions to another mic, and seems to prioritize any external mic over the internal mic.

There is no way to adjust mic volume, although GoToWebinar seems to use automatic gain control (AGC) to ensure adequate volume. If you really want to optimize the volume of your calls, consider a preamp with gain control, like the IK Multimedia iRig PRE shown in Figure 12-5. You can learn how to test mic volume in Chapter 12 in the section entitled "Adjusting Mic Volume in iOS."

GoToWebinar will switch to any headphone once you plug it in, and switch back to the internal speaker once it's removed. Use the hardware volume controls on the mobile device to adjust output volume.

# GoToWebinar on Android

On the Android platform, GoToWebinar has very few user-configurable options, whether within GoToWebinar, in the Android operating system, or via third-party apps. On the version I tested, there was no ability to view others on a webcam, or broadcast from your own webcam on an Android device, although it appeared that this was imminent.

## Choosing the Mic

There's no mic selection option within GoToWebinar. If you have multiple mics attached to your Android device, GoToWebinar seems to use the last mic you added, but it's hard to be sure this works in every instance. If you add a mic during a call, GoToWebinar uses that mic. If you remove the mic–say, by shutting off your Bluetooth device—GoToWebinar automatically transitions to another mic, and seems to prioritize any external mic over the internal mic.

There is no way to adjust mic volume, although GoToWebinar seems to use automatic gain control (AGC) to ensure adequate volume. If you really want to optimize the volume of your calls, consider a preamp with gain control, like the IK Multimedia iRig PRE shown back in Figure 13-5. You can find a discussion of how to test volume on your Android device in Chapter 13 in the section entitled "Adjusting Mic Volume in Android."

GoToWebinar will switch to any headphone once you plug it in, and switch back to the internal speaker once removed. Obviously, you use the hardware volume controls on the mobile device to adjust output volume.

# Chapter 17: Working with On24 Webcast Elite

*Figure 17-1. Configuring On24 Webcast Elite webcam on the Mac.*

On24 Webcast Elite is a self-service, fully featured webinar delivery system that's integrated with leading Customer Relationship Management (CRM) and marketing automation systems to help marketers optimize demand generation, enhance customer engagement and accelerate opportunities in their sales funnel.

As with all these product-oriented chapters, here I focus on how to deliver top-quality audio and video with Webcast Elite.

# Overview

On24 Webcast Elite is a browser-based system that works identically on the Mac and Windows. Although you can consume Webcast Elite webinars on iOS and Android devices, you can't originate from there, so this discussion includes solely computer platforms.

Producing a webinar with Webcast Elite involves two high-level steps. First you configure the webinar, and then you deliver it. While configuring the webinar, you choose video aspect ratio. When delivering the webinar, you select your webcam and mic within the Webcast Elite interface, and then configure your webcam and adjust audio volume using operating system controls. If you call in via telephone, obviously you don't need to worry about your audio settings.

I'll demonstrate all these operations at once, with different paths for Mac and Windows when it comes to webcam configuration and setting mic volume.

# Webcast Elite on Mac and Windows 7

I'll demonstrate on the Mac, although the screens are identical on Windows. Note that while you can customize brightness, contrast, and similar options on the Mac with third-party programs like Mactaris Webcam Settings, you can't with most Windows webcams. For this reason, if you need to customize these appearance-related options with your Windows webcam, you should do this before you run Webcast Elite.

## Choosing Video Aspect Ratio

You choose video resolution and aspect ratio in a window within Webcast Elite called Console Builder, which allows you to customize the player (Figure 17-2). Within the On24 system, I like the 16:9 aspect ratio because it fits better in the webinar player.

*Figure 17-2. Choosing the aspect ratio.*

## Choosing the Webcam and Mic

If you have multiple webcams installed on your computer, you have to choose the desired webcam before getting started. Here's how to do that. Note that you must enter Presentation Manager within the On24 system as a Producer or Presenter and enable Flash to view these controls.

***Step 1. Choosing the webcam.*** On the bottom left in Presentation Manager, click the Webcam drop-down list and choose the desired webcam. There's only one webcam on this Mac so there's no list, but the circled area in Figure 17-3 shows where it would be.

*Figure 17-3. Choosing a webcam. Note that the video is a bit too dark. We'll fix that in a moment.*

**Step 2. Choose the mic.** In the bottom center of Presentation Manager, click the Microphone drop-down list and choose the desired mic (Figure 17-4).

*Figure 17-4. Choosing the mic.*

## Optimizing Webcam Video

The Webcast Elite interface doesn't include configuration options for brightness, contrast, saturation, or similar items. On the Mac, you can use the Webcam Settings program shown in Figure 17-5 to customize your webcam. You can read more about the app in Chapter 6, in a section entitled "Get the Necessary Tools" (around Figure 6-2). As mentioned previously, in Windows, you'll have to use the application that shipped with your webcam to customize appearance before running Webcast Elite.

*Figure 17-5. Optimizing appearance with Webcam Settings on the Mac. Much better now.*

I presented a structured workflow for optimizing these settings (luminance, then color, then sharpness) back in Chapter 6 in a section entitled

"Optimizing Your Webcam Settings." Refer back to that section when adjusting these settings.

>  *Before checking mic volume on either platform, check your speaker or headset volume to make sure it's within a normal range. Otherwise, you might over-crank mic volume simply because the volume on your own speakers or headphones was too low.*

## Setting Mic Volume

As shown in Figure 17-6, the webcam window contains a useful volume meter on the extreme right which you can use to set audio volume. I describe how to set your audio volume in detail in Chapter 9; the CliffsNotes version is that you want volume to top out at about the zone shown in the figure while you're speaking—into the red, but not at the very tippy top. When you're not speaking, you want as little volume showing as possible.

*Figure 17-6. Note the volume meter on the right of the webcam.*

Note that until you actually go live, you won't be able to hear yourself. Once you press the Go Live button on the lower right of the webcam, you can open a preview window from the configuration interface by clicking Preview beneath the webinar (Figure 17-7). Clicking Go Live doesn't actually start the webinar; it just takes the audio and video live so you can preview it.

*Figure 17-7. Opening up a Preview window.*

If you're listening on the same computer that you're speaking on, expect echo and feedback. You should definitely listen with headphones.

## Setting Volume on the Mac

Here's how to set mic volume using the Mac's volume controls. As discussed above, you can perform this using the volume meter on the player (Figure 17-6), or open a preview window (Figure 17-7) and listen in. Either way, you'll probably want to move the Sound Preferences dialog close to the Webcast Elite preview window when performing this work so you can see both windows simultaneously (Figure 17-10).

**Step 1.** Press the Option key and click the sound icon in the menu bar on the upper right, then scroll down and choose Sound Preferences (Figure 17-8).

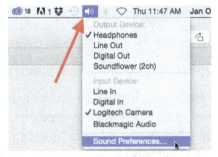

*Figure 17-8. Opening Sound Preferences dialog.*

**Step 2.** In Sound Preferences, (Figure 17-9), click the Input tab on top (if necessary) to view the Input settings, and confirm that the desired mic is selected.

*Figure 17-9. Choose the Input tab and desired mic.*

**Step 3.** In Sound Preferences, drag the input volume slider until the volume is in the target range (Figure 17-10). Here I'm using the volume meter on the player to set initial levels, but after setting levels here, I would definitely go live and preview as a final test.

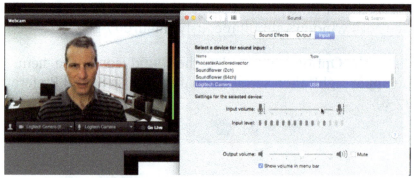

*Figure 17-10. Setting audio volume on the Mac.*

The technique used for setting volume will vary based upon whether you are using a preamp or not, and both are covered in Chapter 11 in sections entitled "Setting Volume—No Preamp" and "Setting Volume—With Preamp." For a general discussion of target volume, see the Section "What's the Target Volume?" in Chapter 9.

## Setting Mic Volume in Windows

Accessing and setting mic volume in Windows involves multiple steps. As discussed above, you can perform this using the volume meter on the player (Figure 17-6), or open a preview window (Figure 17-7) and listen in. Either way, you'll probably want to move the Sound and Microphone

Properties dialogs close to the webcam window when performing this work so you can see the windows simultaneously. Here's the procedure.

**Step 1.** On the bottom right of the task bar, next to the clock, right-click the speaker icon and choose Recording devices (Figure 17-11).

*Figure 17-11. Right-click the speaker icon on the lower right of your Windows desktop.*

**Step 2.** The Sound dialog opens with the Recording tab open (on the left in Figure 17-12). Double-click the mic to open the Microphone Properties dialog (on the right in Figure 17-12).

**Step 3.** In the Microphone Properties dialog, click the Levels tab to expose those controls, and drag the dialog to the right so you can see the volume meters in the Sound dialog (on the left in Figure 17-13). Start with the levels as shown in the figure; note that not all mics will have Microphone Boost.

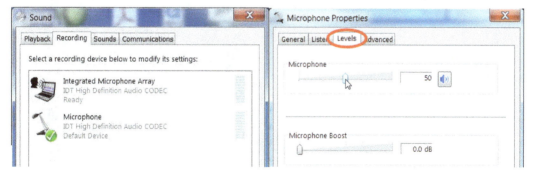

*Figure 17-12. Accessing the microphone volume control in the Levels tab.*

***Step 4.*** In Microphone Properties, drag the Microphone slider until the volume is in the target range (Figure 17-13).

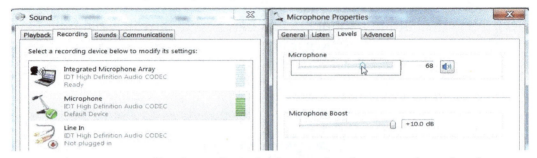

*Figure 17-13. Adjusting volume in the Levels tab. Note volume levels showing on the left next to the Microphone input.*

The technique used will vary based upon whether you are using a preamp or not, and both are covered in Chapter 10 in sections entitled "Setting Volume—No Preamp" and "Setting Volume—With Preamp." For a general discussion of target volume, see the Section "What's the Target Volume?" in Chapter 9.

# Chapter 18: Working with Onstream Webinars

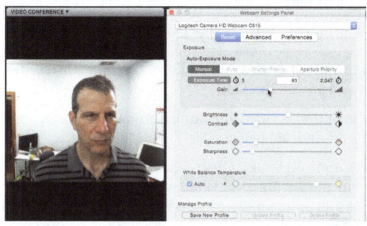

*Figure 18-1. Configuring the Onstream Webinars webcam on the Mac.*

Onstream Media is one of the pioneers in the corporate webcasting market with multiple product entries, including Onstream Webinars, an easy-to-use and affordable self-service system. In this chapter, I discuss how to optimize audio and video quality when using Onstream Webinars.

At the end of the chapter, I briefly discus Onstream's high-end product, Visual Webcaster, and how it differs from Onstream Webinars and other self-service webinar offerings.

# Overview

This chapter is not meant to be a general primer on Onstream Webinars operation. Rather, I focus on how to optimize video and audio quality when using Onstream Webinars in Windows 7, on the Mac, and on iOS and Android mobile devices. Specifically, in this chapter, you will learn:

> • How to optimize video and audio settings for Onstream Webinars in Windows 7 and on the Mac

> • How to optimize video and audio settings for Onstream Webinars on iOS and Android devices.

On computers and notebooks, Onstream Webinars is a Flash application that runs identically on Mac and Windows computers. On Android and iOS devices, it's an app that's not loaded natively on any of the discussed platforms. You should download and install the app before getting started.

Note that as of May 2015, Dolby Voice, which I discuss in a text box entitled, "When Calling into a Webinar" back in Chapter 9 (see Figure 9-10), was not available in the current version of Onstream Webinars. Onstream will add it to the Webinars product sometime during 2015. When it's available, I recommend using it. The quality is fabulous.

# Onstream on Mac and Windows 7

I'll demonstrate primarily on the Mac, although the screens are identical to Windows. I'll be working within Chrome, but operation should be identical in all browsers. Note that while you can customize brightness, contrast, and similar options on the Mac with third-party programs like Mactaris Webcam Settings, you can't with most Windows webcams. For this reason, if you need to customize your Windows webcam, you should do this before starting this process.

## Choosing the Webcam

If you have multiple webcams installed on your computer—virtual or real—you may have to choose the desired webcam before getting started. Here's how to do that. Note that you must enable video in the webinar first to see these screens.

***Step 1.*** On the top left of the Onstream Webinars video window, click the Video Conference drop-down menu and choose Camera settings (Figure 18-2). The Onstream Preferences window opens with the Camera & Video tab selected.

*Figure 18-2. Opening the Onstream Camera settings.*

***Step 2.*** In Onstream Preferences, click the Choose your camera drop-down list and choose the desired webcam (Figure 18-3). Click Apply to close the dialog, or leave it open to customize the webcam configuration.

*Figure 18-3. Choose the desired webcam in the Choose your camera drop-down list.*

## Choosing Video Settings

***Step 1.*** Beneath the camera preview window, Onstream offers a range of settings, including Easy, Professional Video Standards, and Custom. In general, the default 320x240 should suffice for most users, especially when you're getting familiar with the system.

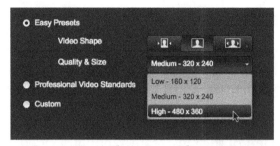

*Figure 18-4. Choosing video settings.*

Here are some other considerations:

• I prefer 4:3 aspect ratios (the middle video shape in Figure 18-4) over 16:9 aspect ratios (extreme right video shape) for webinars unless there are multiple subjects in the frame. With one subject, the space on the sides is typically wasted, and the video frame never seems to fit that neatly into the overall video player.

• I typically use 320 x 240 video because in most cases, the bulk of the screen in my webinars is consumed by PowerPoint slides or similar content. I'll experiment with 480 x 360 resolution or larger if I plan to take the video window to full screen, but larger resolutions require higher outbound bandwidth to retain quality. I discuss the relationship of bandwidth, resolution, and data rate in Chapter 1.

• I wouldn't recommend going beyond 480 x 360 unless you have a very high-quality webcam and know that you have sufficient outbound bandwidth to handle the increased data requirements.

• I wouldn't recommend experimenting with the Professional Video Standards or Custom configuration options unless you really know what you're doing. I'm very conservative with webinars, and I'd rather deliver very high-quality 320 x 240 video with crisp, clear audio than try to hit a home run with high-resolution video and gum up the works.

**Step 2.** When your configuration is complete, click Apply to close the Onstream Preferences window.

## Optimizing Video within the Webcam

The Onstream Webinars interface doesn't include configuration options for brightness, contrast, saturation, or similar items. On the Mac, you can use the Mactaris Webcam Settings app shown in Figure 18-5 to customize your webcam. On Windows, you'll have to use the application that shipped with your webcam to customize appearance before loading Onstream.

I present a structured workflow for optimizing these settings (luminance, then color, then sharpness) back in Chapter 6 in a section entitled "Optimizing Your Webcam Settings." Refer back to that section when adjusting these settings.

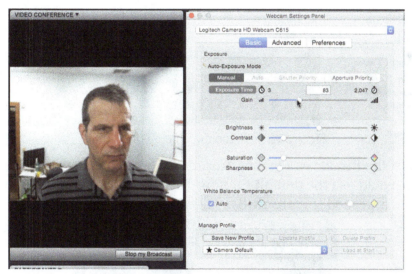

*Figure 18-5. Optimizing appearance in Webcam Settings on the Mac.*

## Choosing the Mic and Adjusting Volume

In Onstream Webinars, if you use computer for audio, you can choose a mic and speakers, and then set volume. Here's how.

**Step 1.** If the Preferences window is still open, click the Audio tab to view the Microphone settings. If not, on the top left of the Onstream video window, click the Video Conference drop-down menu and choose

Microphone settings (Figure 18-6). The Onstream Preferences window opens with the Mic & Speakers tab selected.

*Figure 18-6. Opening the Mic & Speakers tab in Preferences.*

**Step 2.** In the Mic & Speakers tab, click the Choose your microphone drop-down list and choose the desired mic (Figure 18-7).

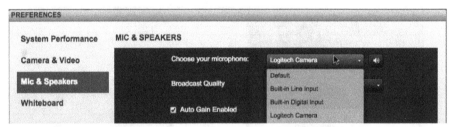

*Figure 18-7. Choosing the desired mic.*

**Step 3.** In the Broadcast Quality drop-down box, choose the desired setting. I would use the default Standard setting unless audio quality is noticeably degraded (Figure 18-8).

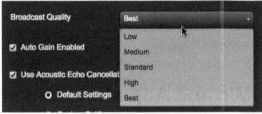

*Figure 18-8. Choosing the desired audio quality.*

**Step 4.** Leave Auto Gain Enabled and Use Acoustic Echo Cancellation at the default settings shown in Figure 18-9. Briefly, Auto Gain will boost mic volume when necessary to send audio with sufficient volume to your viewers. Acoustic Echo Cancellation eliminates echo from other speakers in the conference heard over your device's speakers.

*Figure 18-9. Leave these defaults alone.*

Even though Onstream Webinars offers echo cancellation, keep a headset handy in case echo becomes a problem.

## Setting Audio Volume

With Onstream Webinars, you can run a wizard to check speaker and microphone volume, and adjust volume using operating system controls. I'll assume that you know how to set speaker volume on whichever operating system you're working on, and will show you how to access mic volume controls as we work through the wizard below.

**Step 1.** In the Mic & Speakers Preferences tab, click the Run Sound Check button (Figure 18-10). The Sound Check dialog opens to the Speaker Volume window (Figure 18-11).

*Figure 18-10. Starting the sound check wizard.*

**Step 2.** In the Sound Check dialog, click Play Sound (Figure 18-11). This will start music playing. While it's playing, you can adjust speaker volume using the appropriate controls for your operating system.

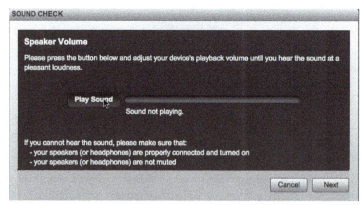

*Figure 18-11. Click Play Sound to start the music and set speaker volume.*

**Step 3.** The Play Sound button converts to the Stop Sound button while the music is playing. Once you have speaker volume adjusted, click Stop Sound, and then Next on the bottom right of the dialog to move to the Microphone Training Window (Figure 18-12).

**Step 4.** Click the Microphone drop-down list and choose your mic.

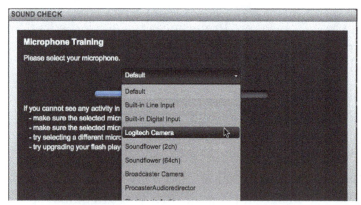

*Figure 18-12. Choosing the desired mic.*

**Step 5.** Once you choose your mic, it's time to adjust the input volume, which you'll do differently based upon the operating system. Note that you can use the volume meter in the Sound Check dialog as a guide while setting mic volume. Let's start with the Mac.

## Setting Mic Volume on the Mac

Here's how to set mic volume using the Mac's volume controls.

**Step 1.** Press the Option key and click the sound icon in the menu bar on the upper right, then scroll down and choose Sound Preferences (Figure 18-13). OS X opens the Sound Preferences, open to the Output tab.

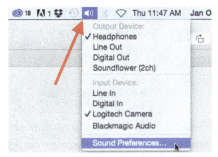

*Figure 18-13. Opening Sound Preferences dialog.*

**Step 2.** In Sound Preferences (Figure 18-14), click the Input tab on top to view the Input settings, and confirm that the desired mic is selected.

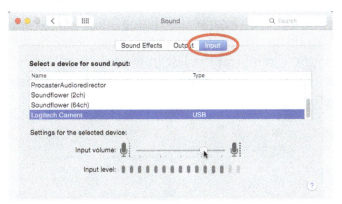

*Figure 18-14. Drag the Input volume to the desired level.*

**Step 3.** In Sound preferences, drag the input volume slider until the volume is in the target range (Figure 18-14). The technique used will vary based upon whether you are using a preamp or not. Both are covered in Chapter 11 in sections entitled "Setting Volume—No Preamp" and "Setting Volume—With Preamp." For a general discussion of target volume, see the Section "What's the Target Volume?" in Chapter 9.

## Setting Mic Volume in Windows

Accessing and setting mic volume in Windows involves multiple steps. Here's the procedure.

**Step 1.** On the bottom right of the task bar, next to the clock, right-click the speaker icon and choose Recording Devices (Figure 18-15).

*Figure 18-15. Right-click the speaker icon on the lower right of your Windows desktop.*

**Step 2.** The Sound dialog opens with the Recording Tab open (on the left in Figure 18-16). Double-click the mic to open the Microphone Properties dialog (on the right in Figure 18-16).

**Step 3.** In the Microphone Properties dialog, click the Levels tab to expose those controls, and drag the dialog to the right so you can see the volume meters in the Sound dialog (on the left in Figure 18-17). Start with the levels as shown in the Figure; note that not all mics will have Microphone Boost.

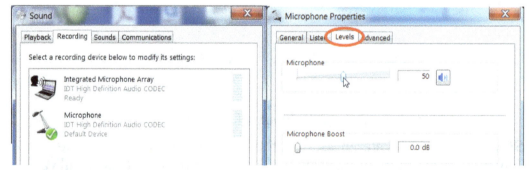

*Figure 18-16. Adjusting mic volume in the Levels tab.*

**Step 4.** In Microphone Properties, drag the Microphone slider until the volume is in the target range (Figure 18-17). The technique used will vary based upon whether you are using a preamp or not, and both are covered in

Chapter 10 in sections entitled "Setting Volume—No Preamp" and "Setting Volume—With Preamp." For a general discussion of target volume, see the Section "What's the Target Volume?" in Chapter 9.

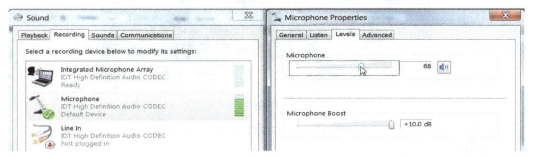

*Figure 18-17. Adjusting volume in the Levels tab. Note volume levels on the left next to the Microphone input. You can also use the meter on Onstream's Microphone Training dialog (Figure 18-18).*

## Resuming the Onstream Wizard

Again, note that while setting volume, you can use the volume meter in the Onstream wizard for guidance (Figure 18-18).

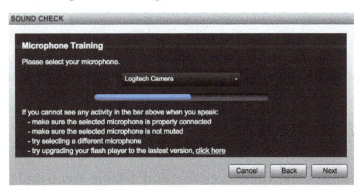

*Figure 18-18. Note the volume meter in the dialog.*

***Step 1.*** Once volume is set at the appropriate level, click Next to move to the Microphone Playback dialog. Using the controls in this dialog, you'll be able to record and play back audio, so you can gauge volume and clarity.

*Figure 18-19. The Microphone Playback dialog.*

• Press the Record button and start speaking. Click the Stop button after 10 to 15 seconds.

• Click the Play button to hear your recorded audio. If volume and clarity are good, click the Finish button to close the dialog and return to the Mic & Speaker Preferences window. If there are issues, click Back and re-test speaker and microphone volumes.

**Step 2.** When your audio configuration is complete, click Apply to close the Preferences dialog.

If you're having audio-related issues in Windows, check Chapter 10 for debugging tips. On the Mac, check Chapter 11.

## Onstream on iOS

With the iOS app, while you can enable and disable audio and video, there are very few additional configuration options. Regarding the webcam, you can switch between front and back cameras, but otherwise, there are no webcam configurations for exposure or white balance controls. This makes lighting critical when making video calls via Onstream Webinars on this platform. Check Chapter 5 for simple, inexpensive techniques you can use to ensure the best possible lighting.

## Choosing the Mic

There's no mic selection option in the Onstream iOS app. If you have multiple mics attached to your iOS device, Onstream will use the last mic you added. If you add a mic during a webinar, Onstream uses that mic; if you remove the mic, Onstream automatically transitions to another mic and prioritizes any external mic over the internal mic.

There is no way to adjust mic volume. If you really want to optimize the volume of your calls, consider a preamp with gain control, like the IK Multimedia iRig PRE shown in Figure 12-5. You can learn how to test mic volume in Chapter 12 in the section "Adjusting Mic Volume in iOS."

Onstream Webinars will switch to any headphone once you plug it in, and switch back to the internal speaker once it's removed. Use the hardware volume controls on the mobile device to adjust output volume.

# Onstream on Android

With the Android app, while you can enable and disable audio and video, there are very few additional configuration options. Regarding the webcam, you can switch between front and back cameras, but otherwise, there are no webcam configurations for exposure or white balance controls. This makes lighting critical when making video calls via Onstream on this platform. Check Chapter 5 for simple, inexpensive techniques you can use to ensure the best possible lighting.

## Choosing the Mic

There's no mic selection option in the Onstream Android app. If you have multiple mics attached to your Android device, Onstream will use the last mic that you added. If you add a mic during a webinar, Onstream uses that mic; if you remove the mic, Onstream automatically transitions to another mic and prioritizes any external mic over the internal mic.

There is no way to adjust mic volume. If you really want to optimize the volume of your calls, consider a preamp with gain control, like the IK Multimedia iRig PRE shown back in Figure 13-5. You can find a discussion of how to test volume on your Android device in Chapter 13 in the section "Adjusting Mic Volume in Android."

Onstream will switch to any headphone once you plug it in, and switch back to the internal speaker once removed. Use the hardware volume controls on the mobile device to adjust output volume.

## Onstream Visual Webcaster

Onstream Media's flagship product is a webcasting platform called Visual Webcaster. I have used it for multiple webinars, and you can find my review at bit.ly/OS_VW. As compared to the Onstream Webinars system, it is designed for larger audiences and offers more bells and whistles including high-resolution video, customizable players, enhanced security, and extensive analytics.

On the delivery side, Visual Webcaster utilizes the Akamai content distribution network to ensure the delivery of very high-quality audio/video to an unlimited audience, as opposed to the proprietary server networks used by some other conferencing products that are limited by audience size and quality. Although Visual Webcaster is more expensive, it's a high-touch, higher-quality experience than Onstream Webinars and a nice option to have when you really need to make a strong impression.

# Chapter 19: Working with Skype

*Figure 19-1. Choosing the webcam in Skype.*

According to Wikipedia, Skype has more than 660 million worldwide users. To curry favor with this expansive group (if only 0.001 percent of them buy this book, I can send my daughters to college!), here's a chapter on optimizing video and audio quality with Skype on Windows, Mac, iOS and Android.

# Overview

This chapter is not meant to be a general primer on Skype operation. Rather, I focus on how to optimize video and audio quality when using Skype in Windows 7, on the Mac, and on iOS and Android mobile devices. Specifically, in this chapter, you will learn:

- How to optimize video and audio settings for Skype on Windows

- How to make a test call on Windows

- How to optimize video and audio settings for Skype on the Mac

- How to make a test call on the Mac

- How to optimize video and audio settings for Skype on iOS devices

- How to make a test call on iOS devices

- How to optimize video and audio settings for Skype on Android devices

- How to make a test call on Android devices.

Note that Skype is a program or app that's not loaded natively on any of the discussed platforms. You should download and install the program before getting started.

As a caveat, Skype is a fast-moving application, and mobile apps, in particular, are in a constant state of flux. I apologize if the Skype app you're using differs significantly from what's shown here. Please contact me at jan@thewebcambook.com for any particularly egregious errors or omissions, or contact me through www.thewebcambook.com.

# Skype on Windows

I'll demonstrate on Windows 7, since it owns the dominant share of Windows users. In Windows, Skype added the ability to configure audio and video settings from within Skype, which simplifies these operations.

## Choosing the Webcam

**Step 1.** In Skype, choose Tools > Options. The Skype Options window opens.

*Figure 19-2. Opening the Skype Options window.*

**Step 2.** In the menu panel on the left of the Options window, click Video settings (Figure 19-3).

**Step 3.** Click the Select webcam atop the video window (if necessary) and choose the appropriate webcam (Figure 19-3).

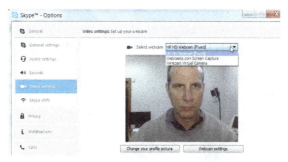

*Figure 19-3. Choosing a webcam in Skype's Options window.*

## Optimizing Video Settings

**Step 1.** In the Skype Options window (Figure 19-3), click the Webcam settings button beneath the video window. Skype opens the Video Capture Filter Properties window (Figure 19-4).

I presented a structured workflow for optimizing these settings (luminance, then color, then sharpness) back in Chapter 6 in a section entitled "Optimizing Your Webcam Settings." Refer back to that section when adjusting these settings.

*Figure 19-4. The Video Capture Filter Properties window.*

*The name of the window that opens when you click the Webcam settings button in Figure 19-3 will likely be different from that shown in Figure 19-4, and the controls will be different depending on your webcam. Refer back to Chapter 6 to learn how to optimize these controls.*

## Choosing a Mic and Adjusting Volume

***Step 1.*** In the menu panel on the left of the Options window, click Audio settings (Figure 19-5).

*Figure 19-5. The Audio settings window.*

***Step 2.*** In the Microphone drop-down list, choose your mic (Figure 19-5).

***Step 3.*** Beneath the Microphone drop-down list, do one of the following:

- Select the Automatically adjust microphone setting checkbox and let Skype adjust mic volume

- Deselect the checkbox and manually set audio volume.

*Figure 19-6. Choosing between automatic and manual mic volume control.*

To learn how to set the appropriate volume, read Chapter 9—particularly the section entitled "Adjusting Volume."

## Choosing Speakers and Adjusting Volume

***Step 1.*** Open the Options window and click Audio settings as described in Steps 1 and 2 of the previous exercise. In the Speakers drop-down list, choose the desired speakers (Figure 19-7).

*Figure 19-7. Choosing the desired speakers.*

***Step 2.*** Beneath the Speakers drop-down list, do one of the following:

- Select the Automatically adjust microphone setting checkbox and let Skype adjust mic volume

- Deselect the checkbox and manually set audio volume.

*Figure 19-8. Choosing between automatic and manual speaker volume control.*

## Making a Test Call

Test calls in Skype are a great way to learn if your mic is loud enough and if your speaker settings are appropriate. I place a test call before almost every important call, just to make sure my audio settings are optimized. Here's how to place a test call in Windows.

**Step 1.** In the Skype menu, choose Contacts > Contact Lists > Skype to show your Skype contacts list.

**Step 2.** Click to select the contact Echo / Sound Test Services (on the lower left of Figure 19-9). If this contact isn't listed, check bit.ly/Skype_test. See the tip after the Android section for more.

*Figure 19-9. Making a test call in Skype.*

**Step 3.** Click the phone icon next to Echo / Sound Test Service to place a voice call (on the upper right of Figure 19-9). Video calls are not permitted.

**Step 4.** Follow the instructions (and enjoy the crisp English accent).

*Note that you can and should adjust the mic and speaker controls shown in Figures 19-6 and 19-8 during the call to optimize mic and speaker settings. When trying new gear for the first time, expect to make a few test calls until you get it right.*

# Skype on The Mac

On the Mac, you choose your webcam and mic within the Skype interface, but optimize video quality and adjust mic volume outside the program.

## Choosing the Webcam

***Step 1.*** In Skype, choose Skype > Preferences. Skype Preferences opens.

*Figure 19-10. Opening Skype Preferences.*

***Step 2.*** In the menu panel atop the Preferences window, click Audio/Video (Figure 19-11).

***Step 3.*** If necessary, choose the appropriate camera in the Camera drop-down list (Figure 19-11).

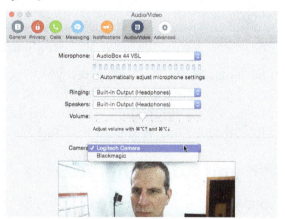

*Figure 19-11. Choosing a webcam in Skype Preferences.*

## Optimizing Your Webcam Settings

As mentioned, the Skype interface doesn't include any webcam optimizations. If you need to adjust brightness, color, or sharpness, I recommend Webcam Settings from Mactaris, which you can read about at bit.ly/web_set. Here's a close-up view of the main Webcam Setting controls (Figure 19-12).

*Figure 19-12. The primary controls in the Webcam Settings program.*

If you use Webcam Settings or another program, your controls will vary by webcam and program. I presented a structured workflow for optimizing these settings (luminance, then color, then sharpness) back in Chapter 6 in a section entitled "Optimizing Your Webcam Settings."

## Choosing a Mic and Adjusting Volume

**Step 1.** In Skype, choose Skype > Preferences. Skype Preferences opens (Figure 19-10).

**Step 2.** In the menu panel atop the Preferences window, click Audio/Video (Figure 19-13).

**Step 3.** If necessary, choose the appropriate mic in the Microphone drop-down list (Figure 19-13).

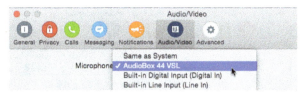

*Figure 19-13. Choosing a mic in the Microphone drop-down list.*

**Step 4.** Beneath the Microphone drop-down list, do one of the following:

• Select the Automatically adjust microphone setting checkbox and let Skype adjust mic volume

• Deselect the checkbox and manually set audio volume.

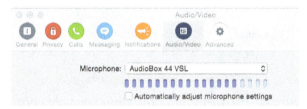

*Figure 19-14. Choosing between automatic and manual mic volume control.*

If you choose manual volume control, you'll do this in Sound Preferences. You can learn how to open Sound Preferences in a section entitled "Choosing a Mic in OS X" in Chapter 11, specifically Figure 11-6 (or press the Option key and click the sound icon in the menu bar). The next two sections in that chapter cover setting volume. As a precursor, to learn how to set the appropriate volume, you might want to read Chapter 9— particularly the section entitled "Adjusting Volume."

## Choosing Speakers and Adjusting Volume

**Step 1.** Open Audio/Video preferences as described in Steps 1 and 2 of the previous exercise. In the Speakers drop-down list, choose the desired speakers (Figure 19-15).

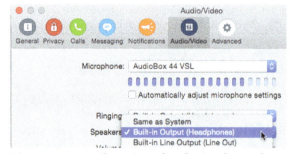

*Figure 19-15. Choosing the desired speakers.*

**Step 2.** Beneath the Speakers drop-down list, you can adjust speaker volume by dragging the volume slider, or via keyboard shortcuts shown in Figure 19-16.

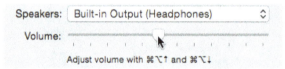

*Figure 19-16. Manually adjusting speaker volume.*

## Making a Test Call

Test calls help you learn if your mic is loud enough and if your speaker settings are appropriate. I place a test call before most important calls to ensure that my audio settings are optimized. Here's how on the Mac.

**Step 1.** In Skype, click Contacts to open your contacts (Figure 19-17).

**Step 2.** Navigate to and hover your pointer over Skype test call. Click Call when the button appears (Figure 19-17). Skype initiates the call.

*Figure 19-17. Making a test call in Skype.*

***Step 3.*** Follow the instructions (and enjoy the crisp English accent).

*Note that you can and should adjust the mic and speaker controls during the call to optimize mic and speaker settings. When trying new gear for the first time, expect to make a few test calls until you get it right.*

# Skype on iOS

On the iOS platform, Skype has very few user-configurable options, whether within Skype, in the iOS operating system, or via third-party apps. I'm demonstrating operation from an iPhone 6, which should be similar, but not identical, to iPad operation.

Regarding the webcam, you can switch between front and back cameras, but otherwise, there are no webcam configurations for exposure or white balance controls. This makes lighting critical when making video calls via Skype. Check Chapter 5 for simple, inexpensive techniques you can use to ensure the best possible lighting.

## Choosing the Mic

There's no mic selection option in Skype. If you have multiple mics attached to your iOS device, Skype seems to use the last mic that you added, but it's hard to be sure this works in every instance. If you add a mic during a call, Skype uses that mic. If you remove the mic—say, by shutting off your Bluetooth device—Skype automatically transitions to another mic, and seems to prioritize any external mic over the internal mic.

There is no way to adjust mic volume, although Skype seems to use automatic gain control (AGC) to ensure adequate volume. If you really want to optimize the volume of your calls, consider a preamp with gain control, like the IK Multimedia iRig PRE shown in Figure 12-5. You can learn how to test mic volume in Chapter 12 in the section "Adjusting Mic Volume in iOS."

Skype will switch to any headphone once you plug it in, and switch back to the internal speaker once it's removed. Use the hardware volume controls on the mobile device to adjust output volume.

## Making a Test Call

Test calls are great on the iOS platforms because mic volume is a consistent concern. Here's how to make a test call on iOS devices.

**Step 1.** In Skype, open your contacts list (Figure 19-18).

**Step 2.** Navigate to and click Echo / Sound Test Service (Figure 19-18), which will take you to the call screen. If this contact isn't listed, check bit.ly/Skype_test. See the tip after the Android section for more.

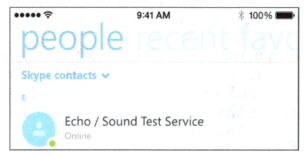

*Figure 19-18. Making a test call in Skype.*

**Step 3.** Click the phone icon on the bottom of the screen to start the call.

**Step 4.** Follow the instructions (and enjoy the crisp English accent).

# Skype on Android

On the Android platform, Skype has very few user-configurable options, whether within Skype, in the Android operating system, or via third-party apps. I'm demonstrating operation on a Samsung Galaxy Nexus 10, which should be similar, but not identical, to Android smartphone operation.

Regarding the webcam, obviously there's only one, so you don't need to choose it. As far as I'm aware, there are no webcam configuration options for exposure or white balance controls on the tablet. This makes lighting extremely important when making video calls via Skype. Check Chapter 5 for simple, inexpensive techniques you can use to ensure the best possible lighting.

## Choosing the Mic

There's no mic selection option within Skype. If you have multiple mics attached to your Android device, Skype seems to use the last mic that you added, but it's hard to be sure this works in every instance. If you add a mic during a call, Skype uses that mic. If you remove the mic—say, by shutting off your Bluetooth device—Skype automatically transitions to another mic, and seems to prioritize any external mic over the internal mic.

There is no way to adjust mic volume, although Skype seems to use automatic gain control (AGC) to ensure adequate volume. If you really want to optimize the volume of your calls, consider a preamp with gain control, like the IK Multimedia iRig PRE shown back in Figure 13-5. You can find a discussion of how to test volume on your Android device in Chapter 13 in the section "Adjusting Mic Volume in Android."

Skype will switch to any headphone once you plug it in, and switch back to the internal speaker once removed. Obviously, you use the hardware volume controls on the mobile device to adjust output volume.

## Making a Test Call

Test calls are great because mic volume is a consistent concern. Here's how to make a test call on Android devices.

**Step 1.** In Skype, open your contacts (Figure 19-19).

**Step 2.** Navigate to and choose the Echo / Sound Test Service (Figure 19-19), which will take you to the call screen. If this contact isn't listed, check the tip immediately below this section.

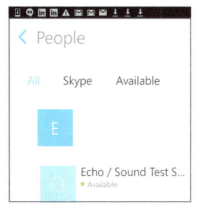

*Figure 19-19. Making a test call in Skype.*

**Step 3.** Click the phone icon on the bottom of the screen to start the call.

**Step 4.** Follow the instructions (and enjoy the crisp English accent).

*Figure 19-20. Finding the Echo / Sound Test Services contact.*

*If the contact Echo / Sound Test Services isn't in your contact list, search for echo123 on Skype (Figure 19-20). Do not search for Echo / Sound Test Services, as there are dozens of these contacts who are mostly not affiliated with Skype. Check bit.ly/Skype_test if you're having trouble finding the number.*

# Chapter 20: Working with TalkPoint Convey

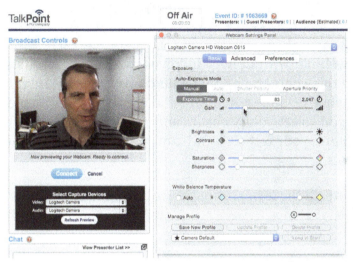

*Figure 20-1. Configuring the TalkPoint Convey webcam on the Mac.*

TalkPoint Convey is a self-service, fully featured webinar delivery system that's ideal for marketing, communications and sales-oriented webinars. Basically, any time you want to make a great impression and not spend a fortune doing it, you should consider Convey. You can read my review of the system at bit.ly/Ozer_Convey.

As with all these product-oriented chapters, here I focus on how to deliver top-quality audio and video with Convey.

# Overview

TalkPoint Convey is a browser-based system that works identically on the Mac and Windows. Although you can consume Convey webinars on iOS and Android devices, you can't originate from there, so this discussion is based solely on computer platforms.

Producing a webinar with Convey involves two high-level steps. First you configure the webinar, and then you deliver it. While configuring the webinar, you choose video resolution and aspect ratio. When delivering the webinar, you select your webcam and mic within the Convey interface, and you configure your webcam and adjust audio volume using operating system controls.

I'll demonstrate all these operations once, with different paths for Mac and Windows when it comes to webcam configuration and setting mic volume.

# Convey on Mac and Windows 7

I'll demonstrate primarily on the Mac, although the screens are identical to Windows. Note that while you can customize brightness, contrast, and similar options on the Mac with third-party programs like Mactaris Webcam Settings, you can't with most Windows webcams. For this reason, if you need to customize these appearance-related options with your Windows webcam, you should do this before you run Convey.

## Choosing Video Resolution and Aspect Ratio

You choose video resolution and aspect ratio when customizing player and branding options (Figure 20-2). Here are some thoughts to consider when choosing these parameters:

> • I typically use 320 x 240 video in my webinars because in most cases, the bulk of the screen contains PowerPoint slides or similar content. I'll experiment with 480 x 360 resolution or larger if I

plan to take the video window to full screen, but larger resolutions require higher outbound bandwidth to retain quality. I discuss the relationship of bandwidth, resolution, and data rate in Chapter 1.

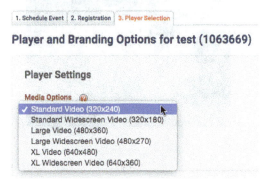

*Figure 20-2. Choosing resolution and aspect ratio.*

• I prefer 4:3 aspect ratios (320 x 240, 480 x 360, 640 x 480) over 16:9 aspect ratios (320 x 180, 480 x 270, 640 x 360) for webinars unless there are multiple subjects in the frame. With one subject, the space on the sides is typically wasted and just takes up extra space.

• I wouldn't go beyond 480 x 360 unless you have a very high-quality webcam and know that you have sufficient outbound bandwidth to handle the increased data requirements. I'm very conservative with webinars, and I'd rather deliver very high-quality 320 x 240 video with crisp, clear audio than try to hit a home run with high-resolution video and gum up the works.

## Choosing the Webcam

If you have multiple webcams installed on your computer—virtual or real—you may have to choose the desired webcam before getting started. Here's how to do that. Note that you must enter Convey's Live Studio interface to view these controls.

***Step 1.*** In the Live Studio interface, click Preview beneath the video window (Figure 20-3). A Select Capture Devices box appears with two drop-down lists: one for video and the other for audio (Figure 20-4).

*Figure 20-3. Opening the select capture device interface.*

**Step 2.** In the Select Capture Devices box, click the Video drop-down list and choose the desired webcam.

*Figure 20-4. Choosing the webcam.*

**Step 3.** In the Select Capture Devices box, click the Audio drop-down list and choose the desired mic.

*Figure 20-5. Choosing the mic.*

**Step 4.** In the Select Capture Devices box, click the Refresh Preview button. This updates the video in the preview window, but it doesn't connect the audio, so you can't yet check mic volume.

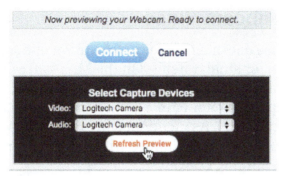

*Figure 20-6. Click Refresh Preview to update the
webcam selection in the preview window.*

**Step 5.** Click the Connect button to preview both audio and video in the preview window. Convey will then connect the audio/video stream to their servers and send a live stream back to Live Studio (Figure 20-7).

**Step 6.** In the video preview window, click Listen to Presenter Audio to hear the audio you are broadcasting (Figure 20-7). As you can see in the figure, headphones are useful when customizing your mic settings. Now you're ready to customize your video settings (on the Mac) and mic volume.

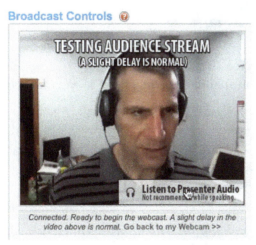

*Figure 20-7. Click Listen to Presenter Audio to hear your audio.
Then you can set the mic volume.*

## Optimizing Webcam Video

The Convey interface doesn't include configuration options for brightness, contrast, saturation, or similar items. On the Mac, you can use the Webcam Settings app shown in Figure 20-8 to customize your webcam. You can read more about the app in Chapter 6, in a section entitled "Get the Necessary Tools" (around Figure 6-2). As mentioned previously, in Windows, you'll have to use the application that shipped with your webcam to customize appearance before running Convey.

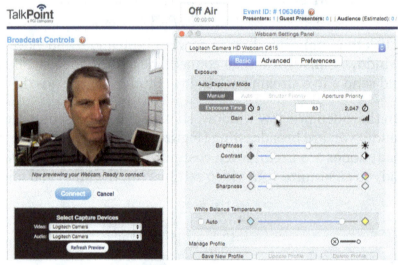

*Figure 20-8. Optimizing appearance in Webcam Settings on the Mac.*

I presented a structured workflow for optimizing these settings (luminance, then color, then sharpness) back in Chapter 6 in a section entitled "Optimizing Your Webcam Settings." Refer back to that section when adjusting these settings.

> *tip* *Before checking mic volume on either platform, check your speaker or headset volume to make sure it's within a normal range. Otherwise, you might over-crank mic volume simply because the volume on your own speakers or headphones was too low.*

# Setting Mic Volume on the Mac

Here's how to set mic volume using the Mac's volume controls. Note that you'll perform this after opening the live preview window (Figure 20-7). You'll probably want to move the Sound Preferences dialog close to the Convey preview window when performing this work so you can see both windows simultaneously.

***Step 1.*** Press the Option key and click the sound icon in the menu bar on the upper right, then scroll down and choose Sound Preferences (Figure 20-9).  OS X opens the Sound preferences, open to the Output tab.

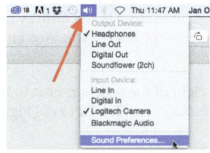

*Figure 20-9. Opening Sound Preferences dialog.*

***Step 2.*** In Sound Preferences (Figure 20-10), click the Input tab on top (if necessary) to view the Input settings, and confirm that the desired mic is selected.

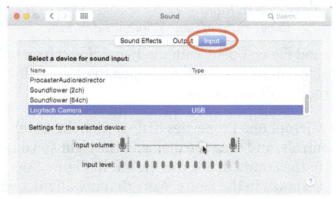

*Figure 20-10. Drag the Input volume to the desired level.*

**Step 3.** In Sound Preferences, drag the input volume slider until the volume is in the target range (Figure 20-10). The technique used will vary based upon whether you are using a preamp or not, and both are covered in Chapter 11 in sections entitled "Setting Volume—No Preamp" and "Setting Volume—With Preamp." For a general discussion of target volume, see the section "What's the Target Volume?" in Chapter 9.

## Setting Mic Volume in Windows

Accessing and setting mic volume in Windows involves multiple steps. Note that you'll perform this after opening the live preview window (Figure 20-7). You'll probably want to move the Sound preferences and Microphone Properties dialogs close to the Convey preview window when performing this work so you can sell the windows simultaneously. Here's the procedure.

**Step 1.** On the bottom right of the task bar, next to the clock, right-click the speaker icon and choose Recording Devices (Figure 20-11).

*Figure 20-11. Right-click the speaker icon on the lower right of your Windows desktop.*

**Step 2.** The Sound dialog opens with the Recording tab open (on the left in Figure 20-12). Double-click the mic to open the Microphone Properties dialog (on the right in Figure 20-12).

**Step 3.** In the Microphone Properties dialog, click the Levels tab to expose those controls, and drag the dialog to the right so you can see the volume meters in the Sound dialog (on the left in Figure 20-13). Start with the levels as shown in the figure. Note that not all mics will have Microphone Boost.

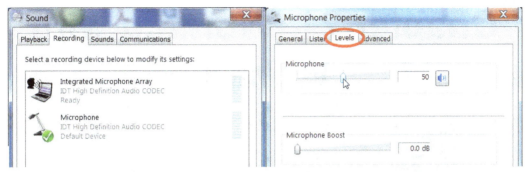

*Figure 20-12. Accessing the microphone volume control in the Levels tab.*

**Step 4.** In Microphone Properties, drag the Microphone slider until the volume is in the target range (Figure 20-13).

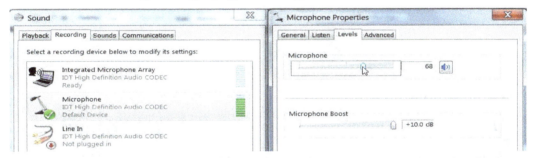

*Figure 20-13. Adjusting volume in the Levels tab. Note volume levels showing on the left next to the Microphone input.*

The technique used will vary based upon whether you are using a preamp or not, and both are covered in Chapter 10 in sections entitled "Setting Volume—No Preamp" and "Setting Volume—With Preamp." For a general discussion of target volume, see the section "What's the Target Volume in Chapter 9.

# Chapter 21: Working with WebEx

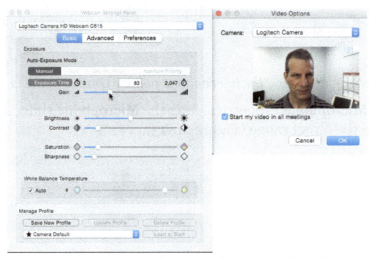

*Figure 21-1. Configuring my webcam on the Mac with Webcam Settings.*

According to the Cisco WebEx manual, WebEx "automatically adjusts video to the highest quality for each participant according to the computer capabilities and network bandwidth." So if you take the time to optimize the appearance of your video, every viewer should benefit.

# Overview

This chapter is not meant to be a general primer on WebEx operation. Rather, I focus on how to optimize video and audio quality when using WebEx on Windows 7, on the Mac, and on iOS and Android mobile devices. Specifically, in this chapter, you will learn:

- How to optimize video and audio for WebEx on Windows 7

- How to optimize video and audio for WebEx on the Mac

- How to optimize video and audio for WebEx on iOS devices

- How to optimize video and audio for WebEx on Android devices.

WebEx is a plug-in or app that's not native on any of the discussed platforms. Please install the app or plug-in before getting started.

As a caveat, WebEx is a fast-moving application, and mobile apps, in particular, are in a constant state of flux. I apologize in advance if the WebEx app or plug-in you're using differs significantly from what's shown here. Please contact me at jan@thewebcambook.com for any particularly egregious errors or omissions, or contact me through www.thewebcambook.com.

# WebEx on Windows

I'll demonstrate on Windows 7, since it still has the dominant share of Windows users. I'll demonstrate using Google Chrome with the WebEx extension installed and enabled. If you're working in a different browser, you should see the same screens as shown below, but I can't guarantee it.

## Choosing the Webcam

If you have multiple webcams installed on your computer—virtual or real—you may have to choose the desired webcam before getting started. Here's how to do that. Note that you must enable video in the meeting or conference first to see these screens.

**Step 1.** On the top right of the WebEx Meetings interface, click the gear icon (Figure 21-2). The Video Options window opens.

*Figure 21-2. Opening the WebEx Video Options window.*

**Step 2.** In the Video Options dialog, click the Camera drop-down list and choose the desired webcam (Figure 21-3). Click OK to close the dialog or leave it open to customize the webcam configuration.

*Figure 21-3. Choose the desired webcam in the Camera drop-down list.*

## Optimizing Video Settings

**Step 1.** In the WebEx Video Options window (Figure 21-3), click the Advanced Options button to the right of the video window. WebEx opens the configuration window for your webcam (Figure 21-4).

I presented a structured workflow for optimizing these settings (luminance, then color, then sharpness) back in Chapter 6 in a section entitled "Optimizing Your Webcam Settings." Refer back to that section when adjusting these settings.

HP HD Webcam [Fixed] Properties

VideoProcAmp | CameraControl |

| | | | Auto |
|---|---|---|---|
| Brightness | | 0 | ☐ |
| Contrast | | 32 | ☐ |
| Hue | | 0 | ☐ |
| Saturation | | 64 | ☐ |
| Sharpness | | 3 | ☐ |
| Gamma | | 100 | ☐ |
| White Balance | | 6500 | ☑ |
| Backlight Comp | | 0 | ☐ |

PowerLine Frequency    Auto ▼
(Anti Flicker)

Default

*Figure 21-4. The Webcam Properties window.*

**tip** *The name of the window that opens when you click the Advanced Options button in Figure 21-3 will likely be different from that shown in Figure 21-4 depending on your webcam, and the controls will be different. Refer back to Chapter 6 to learn how to optimize these controls.*

## Choosing the Mic and Adjusting Volume

In WebEx, if you call in using the computer, you can choose a mic and speakers, and set volume in the Test Computer Audio dialog. Here's how.

**Step 1.** In the Audio Connection dialog, click the Test computer audio link beneath Using Computer for Audio (Figure 21-5). The Test Computer Audio dialog opens. If you've already chosen Computer Audio, click the More button to see the Test computer audio link.

‹    Audio Connection    ×

↪  I Will Call In

✓  **Using Computer for Audio**
   Test computer audio

*Figure 21-5. Click Test computer audio to open the Test Computer Audio dialog.*

**Step 2.** In the Test Computer Audio dialog, click the Microphone drop-down list and choose the desired mic (Figure 21-6).

*Figure 21-6. Choosing the desired mic.*

**Step 3.** Beneath the Microphone drop-down list, do one of the following:

• Select the Automatically adjust volume checkbox and let WebEx adjust mic volume.

• Deselect the checkbox, and manually set audio volume (recommended).

*Figure 21-7. Choosing between automatic and manual mic volume control.*

**Step 4.** Click OK to close the dialog (or leave open to choose the Speaker in the next step).

*tip* *To learn how to set the appropriate volume, read Chapter 9—particularly the section entitled "Adjusting Volume."*

## Choosing the Speaker and Adjusting Volume

**Step 1.** Follow the steps in the previous exercise to open the Test Computer Audio dialog. In the Speaker drop-down list, choose the desired speaker (Figure 21-8).

*Figure 21-8. Choosing the desired speaker.*

**Step 2.** Click the Test button to play the test sounds, and drag the volume slider to the desired level.

**Step 3.** Click OK to close the dialog.

*tip* *Note that WebEx does use echo cancellation, which works well most of the time. As with all conferencing software, however, it pays to keep a headset handy in case echo-related problems arise.*

# WebEx on The Mac

On the Mac, you choose your webcam within the WebEx interface, but optimize video quality outside the plug-in. For audio, you can choose mic and speaker and set volume for both inside the plug-in.

## Choosing the Webcam

**Step 1.** In the WebEx Meetings interface, click the gear icon (Figure 21-9). The Video Options window opens.

*Figure 21-9. Opening the WebEx Video Options window.*

**Step 2.** In the Video Options dialog, click the Camera drop-down list and choose the desired webcam (Figure 21-10). Click OK to close the dialog.

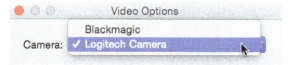

*Figure 21-10. Choosing the Logitech webcam.*

*tip* *Since WebEx can choose the Blackmagic capture device in my Mac Pro, it may recognize a camera attached to the card, a nice higher-quality option when a webcam won't do. See the final section in Chapter 2, "Going Beyond the Webcam," for further discussion of this. Also see the article at bit.ly/HDCAM_MacWebcam, which discusses this precise issue.*

## Optimizing Your Webcam Settings

As mentioned, on the Mac, the WebEx interface doesn't include any webcam optimizations, or at least doesn't seem to on any of the Macs that I've used or tested. If you need to adjust brightness, color, or sharpness, I recommend Webcam Settings from Mactaris, which you can read about at bit.ly/web_set. Here's a close-up view of the basic Webcam Setting controls (Figure 21-11), and in Figure 21-1, I'm using these controls to configure the webcam on my Mac Pro.

*Figure 21-11. The Basic controls in the Webcam Settings program.*

If you use Webcam Settings or another program, your controls will vary by webcam and program. I presented a structured workflow for optimizing these settings (luminance, then color, then sharpness) back in Chapter 6 in a section entitled "Optimizing Your Webcam Settings."

## Choosing the Mic and Adjusting Volume

In WebEx, if you call in using the computer, you can choose a mic and speakers, and set volume in the Test Computer Audio dialog. Here's how.

**Step 1.** In the Audio Connection dialog, click the Test computer audio link beneath Using Computer for Audio (Figure 21-12). The Test Computer Audio dialog opens.

*Figure 21-12. Click Test computer audio to open the Test Computer Audio dialog.*

**Step 2.** In the Test Computer Audio dialog, click the Microphone drop-down list and choose the desired mic (Figure 21-13).

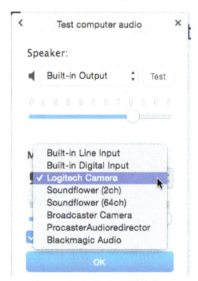

*Figure 21-13. Choosing the desired mic.*

**Step 3.** Beneath the Microphone drop-down list, do one of the following:

• Select the Automatically adjust volume checkbox and let WebEx adjust mic volume.

• Deselect the checkbox, and manually set audio volume (recommended).

*Figure 21-14. Choosing between automatic and manual mic volume control.*

**Step 4.** Click OK to close the dialog (or leave open to choose the Speaker in the next step).

> (tip) *To learn how to set the appropriate volume, read Chapter 9—particularly the section entitled "Adjusting Volume."*

## Choosing the Speaker and Adjusting Volume

**Step 1.** Follow the steps in the previous exercise to open the Test Computer Audio dialog. In the Speaker drop-down list, choose the desired speaker (Figure 21-15).

*Figure 21-15. Choosing the desired speaker.*

**Step 2.** Click the Test button to play the test sounds, and drag the volume slider to the desired level.

# WebEx on iOS

On the iOS platform, WebEx works impressively well (Apple Watch!), but has very few user-configurable options, whether within WebEx, in the iOS operating system, or via third-party apps. Regarding the webcam, you can switch between front and back cameras, but otherwise, there are no webcam configurations for exposure or white balance controls. As far as I'm aware, there are no webcam configurations for exposure or white balance controls on the iOS platform. This makes lighting critical when making video calls via WebEx on this platform. Check Chapter 5 for simple, inexpensive techniques you can use to ensure the best possible lighting.

## Choosing the Mic

There's no mic selection option in the WebEx iOS version. If you have multiple mics attached to your iOS device, WebEx seems to use the last mic you added, but it's hard to be sure this works in every instance. If you add a mic during a call, WebEx uses that mic. If you remove the mic, WebEx automatically transitions to another mic, and seems to prioritize any external mic over the internal mic.

There is no way to adjust mic volume, although WebEx seems to use automatic gain control (AGC) to ensure adequate volume. If you really want to optimize the volume of your calls, consider a preamp with gain control, like the IK Multimedia iRig PRE shown in Figure 12-5. You can learn how to test mic volume in Chapter 12 in the section "Adjusting Mic Volume in iOS."

WebEx will switch to any headphone once you plug it in, and switch back to the internal speaker once it's removed. Use the hardware volume controls on the mobile device to adjust output volume.

# WebEx on Android

On the Android platform, WebEx has very few user-configurable options, whether within WebEx, in the Android operating system, or via third-party apps. Regarding the webcam, obviously there's only one, so you don't need to choose it. As far as I'm aware, there are no webcam configuration options for exposure or white balance controls on Android devices. This makes lighting extremely important when making video calls via WebEx. Check Chapter 5 for simple, inexpensive techniques you can use to ensure the best possible lighting.

## Choosing the Mic

There's no mic selection option in the WebEx Android version. If you have multiple mics attached to your Android device, WebEx seems to use the last mic you added, but it's hard to be sure this works in every instance. If you add a mic during a call, WebEx uses that mic. If you remove the mic, WebEx automatically transitions to another mic, and seems to prioritize any external mic over the internal mic.

There is no way to adjust mic volume, although WebEx seems to use automatic gain control (AGC) to ensure adequate volume. If you really want to optimize the volume of your calls, consider a preamp with gain control, like the IK Multimedia iRig PRE shown back in Figure 13-5. You can find a discussion of how to test volume on your Android device in Chapter 13 in the section "Adjusting Mic Volume in Android."

WebEx will switch to any headphone once you plug it in, and switch back to the internal speaker once removed. Obviously, you use the hardware volume controls on the mobile device to adjust output volume.

# Chapter 22: Getting it Right on Game Day

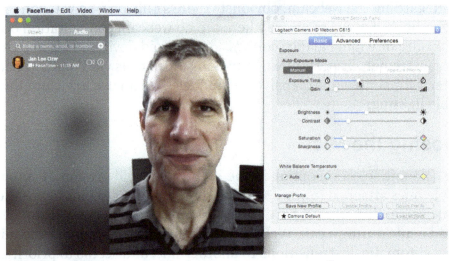

*Figure 22-1. It's time to get your game face on.*

We've spent 21 chapters learning the finer points of audio and videoconferencing; now it's game day, or the day before game day. I'm not about to let a silly slip-up ruin all of our hard work.

So, this chapter presents some checklists you can use to avoid rookie errors that I've seen or made myself over the years.

# Overview

In this chapter, I'll present four sets of checklists, as follows:

- The week before the event
- The day before the event
- The day of the event
- After the event.

Figuring out the scope of this chapter was a tough balancing act. You'd do things differently if you were presenting a webinar to 1,000 participants than you would if you were having a quick video chat with a client or channel partner. So I decided to err on the side of being too careful, rather than too casual.

# The Week Before the Event

Here are some considerations for about a week before the event.

- ***Bandwidth.*** If you're in an office setting, check with your IT department to make sure you have sufficient bandwidth, and take any steps to preserve that bandwidth (see Chapter 1).

- ***Location.*** Identify where you'll hold the conference and reserve that location. Make sure the background is conferencing friendly as discussed in Chapter 3. If you need to reserve further in advance, obviously you should do so.

- ***Equipment.*** Figure out a plan for lighting, sound, and positioning your webcam or mobile phone. Get the gear you need ordered or reserved.

- ***Rehearsal plan.*** For larger events hosted by a webinar provider, there will be a rehearsal. Identify when that will be and make sure all critical parties are available, including all speakers, moderators, planners, marketing folks, and producers.

• ***Redundancy plan.*** If you're running a webinar via a company computer, what happens if the computer fails or you lose bandwidth? What happens if the phone service fails? The odds are very low, but these things happen. Alternatives will vary by service provider and what actually fails, but think through several scenarios and come up with a plan B. For example:

◇ Have a spare laptop handy in case of computer failure.

◇ Have a 4G modem available in case your office LAN goes down.

◇ If you're using a webinar service provider, ask them about backup. If you lose connectivity, you may be able to call in (via a landline of course) and simply have them advance the slides.

# The Day Before the Event

Here are checklists for the day before the event.

## Equipment Check

• Locate all the mics, lights, tripods and other gear you will use for the event. This assumes that you have a rough plan for where all the equipment will go and how you will use it. If not, at least sketch out where the lights will go, since lighting is important and the most complicated.

• Check batteries on any battery-powered devices.

• Check bulbs on any lights with bulbs.

• If possible, get all the gear assembled and tested where you intend to hold the conference. I sleep better if all my gear is set up and known to be working the day before the event.

## Presentation Check

• If you're a presenting with a PowerPoint or Keynote presentation, make sure it's complete.

• Print a copy of the presentation.

• If you're using a webinar system that lets you upload a presentation, upload it now.

• If the system lets viewers download the presentations, upload a copy they can download.

• Make sure you're comfortable with whatever software program you'll be using.

## Bandwidth Check

• If you're working in an office, contact the relevant IT person and confirm the bandwidth has been reserved

## Procedure Check

• Review the invite or other plan for the event. Be sure to:

   ◇ Identify who will place the call or make the connection.

   ◇ Identify which service will be used.

   ◇ Have contact information handy (Skype/FaceTime username, Google Hangouts ID).

   ◇ If necessary, send a connection invite (as with Skype) to make the necessary connections.

## Clothing and Hygiene Check

• Plan what clothing you will wear for the conference, and make sure it's available to grab quickly in the morning.

• Think about morning hygiene for the day of. For me, that means shaving and showering to get my hair together.

• Pack a towel to bring with you, or plan to use paper towels, to wipe any shiny areas on your face or forehead. If you're particularly prone to moisture, consider bringing and applying loose powder.

# The Day of the Event

Large conferences have separate professionals in charge of each aspect of the event: camera, sound, lighting, backdrop, direction, bandwidth monitor, and software operator. All perform critical roles that can make or break conference quality. You probably don't have the benefit of all these folks, so you'll have to perform all the roles yourself.

On game day, thinking of these roles separately simplifies the process for me, so that's how I'll present it.

## 90 Minutes to Go Time

If you're participating in a webinar, most producers will want to get you connected at least an hour before the event. So you have to get all this stuff done before you get connected. For conferences or webinars you're driving yourself, you can start this about an hour before the event.

### Computer/Camera Operator

You'll need the computer and webcam running so you can test other aspects of the production.

• Computer turned on and running. Make sure it's plugged in; do not run on battery.

• Get connected to the internet. Remember wired is preferred over wireless. Turn off your Wi-Fi if necessary.

• Disable all non-essential software—in particular, any programs that might pop up or beep, like Outlook or any messenger programs.

• Check connectivity with Speedtest.net.

- Start the webcam and check rule-of-thirds positioning.

- Once it's time to get connected to the webinar service, do so.

## Lighting Guy or Gal (Gaffer)

Lights can take forever to get set up, so tackle this as soon as possible.

- Lights in position.

- Lights turned on.

- Check for hotspots in the webcam.

## Sound Guy or Gal

- Get audio gear connected.

- Check audio volume.

- Consider making a Skype test call (even if it's not a Skype conference) to verify volumes.

- Have a plan for what happens when speaker needs to use the potty 15 minutes before the event.

- If you're using a computer without a headset, have a headset available in case echoes start to occur.

- Think about noise reduction during the event, particularly for noisy HVAC gear. This may mean pumping up the AC beforehand so you can turn it off and stay comfortable during the event, or turning up the heat in advance during the winter.

## Director

- Check the background. Make sure it's compression friendly.

- Neaten up. Check what's showing in the webcam and remove any papers, coffee cups, cables, gear, or other detritus. You don't want anything distracting in the viewfinder.

- Run through your contingency plan.

## Performer

- Appearance check: Clothing and hair OK?

- Remove extraneous jewelry.

- Have water, coffee or whatever you'll need during the conference.

- Have a mirror and towel available to check for and wipe away shiny spots, or apply loose powder.

- Have a copy of your slides handy, and whatever is needed for your redundancy plan.

- If working with a third-party webinar-hosting provider, have a plan for who will moderate questions at the end of the webinar.

- For webinars, script out the first few statements you'll make. If you're starting the webinar, you need to:

    ◇ Thank attendees (and sponsor).

    ◇ Set parameters (e.g. 45 minute presentation, 15 for Q&A).

    ◇ Discuss what's available in the system software—particularly how to download slides and ask questions.

- If you're just a speaker, you need to:

    ◇ Thank the sponsor and person who introduced you.

    ◇ Thank attendees.

    ◇ Know who you're passing the webinar to once your portion is complete.

- Other items:

    ◇ Formulate some questions yourself in case there are none from the audience.

    ◇ Prepare closing remarks (thanks, future events, calls to action, availability of on-demand version of webinar).

## 15 to 30 Minutes Before the Event

Final preparation time.

### Sound Guy or Gal

- Place Do Not Disturb sign on the office or conference room door.

- Shut AC off.

- Turn off all non-essential equipment, including printers, other computers, etc.

- Make sure all phones are turned off or on silent. Even on vibrate, cell phones can be audible to webinar viewers—not to mention distracting to the speakers.

- Take other steps to make sure the room is as quiet as possible.

### Performer

- Final potty trip; verify appearance one last time.

- Get audio reconnected and test for the final time.

- Check for water, presentation hard copy, and redundancy phone.

- Stay loose. You're going to sound and look great.

# After the Event

Immediately after the event, remember to write down what you'll do better the next time. Your recollections will never be sharper, and you'll be much more inclined to remember and put them to good use for your next presentation.

# Thanks and Good Presenting

Well, that's it. I hope you found the foregoing useful. If so, please spread the word on Amazon, the iBook store, Barnes & Noble, or wherever good books are sold. And if not, well, I'll try harder next time.

If you have any thoughts to share directly, please contact me at jan@thewebcambook.com or through www.thewebcambook.com.

# Index

www.ingramcontent.com/pod-product-compliance
Lightning Source LLC
Chambersburg PA
CBHW080550060326
40689CB00021B/4801